Contents

Acknowledgements

The author wishes to thank the following for their help with the editing and production of the book: Mike Fardon, Mike Gilbert, Rosemarie Griffiths, Claire McCarthy, Jon Moore and Pineapple Publishing. Special thanks go to Roger Petheram, Series Editor, for reading, checking and advising on the development of this workbook.

The publisher is indebted to the Association of Accounting Technicians for its generous help and advice to our authors and editors during the preparation of this text, and for permission to reproduce extracts from published assessment material.

Authors

Janet Brammer has over twelve years' experience lecturing on AAT and ACCA accountancy courses at Norwich City College. She is a Certified Accountant and worked in accountancy practice for a number of years. She has also tutored for the Open University and has written a workbook *Management Information Framework* for the ACCA distance learning scheme. Janet is also co-author of *Active Accounting* and *Managing Performance & Resources Tutorial* from Osborne Books.

Aubrey Penning co-ordinates the AAT courses at Worcester College of Technology, and teaches a range of units including Unit 33 and the two taxation Units. He has over eighteen years experience of teaching accountancy on a variety of courses in Worcester and Gwent. He is a Certified Accountant, and before his move into full-time teaching he worked for the health service, a housing association and a chemical supplier. Aubrey is co-author of *Managing Performance & Resources Tutorial* and *Cash Management & Credit Control* from Osborne Books.

Management Accounting

Workbook

AAT Diploma Pathway Unit 33

Janet Brammer

Aubrey Penning

osborne
BOOKS

Published by Osborne Books Limited
Unit 1B Everoak Estate
Bromyard Road
Worcester WR2 5HP
Tel 01905 748071
Email books@osbornebooks.co.uk
Website www.osbornebooks.co.uk

Design by Richard Holt
Cover image from Getty Images

Printed by the Bath Press, Bath

British Library Cataloguing in Publication Data
A catalogue record for this book is available from the British Library

ISBN 1 905777 08 6

082
9781 905 777 150.

How to use this book

Management Accounting Workbook is designed to be used by Diploma students alongside Osborne Books' *Managing Performance & Resources Tutorial* and is ideal for student use in the classroom, at home and on distance learning courses. Both the Tutorial and the Workbook are suitable for students preparing for assessment on the Diploma Pathway Unit 33 'Management Accounting'.

Management Accounting Workbook is divided into two sections: Workbook Activities and Practice Examinations.

Workbook Activities

Workbook activities are self-contained exercises which are designed to be used to supplement the activities in the tutorial text. Many of them are more extended than the exercises in the tutorial and provide useful practice for students preparing for examinations. There are activities relating to each chapter of the tutorial text.

Practice Examinations

Osborne Books is grateful to the AAT for their kind permission for the reproduction of the AAT Specimen Examinations in this section and selected modified tasks from other Examinations. Note that although the practice examinations (including the specimen paper) are divided into three sections, the AAT has stated that actual examinations may not necessarily follow this format.

answers

The answers to the tasks and exams in the *Workbook* are available in a separate *Tutor Pack*. Contact the Osborne Books Sales Office on 01905 748071 for details of how to obtain the Tutor Pack.

Workbook activities

This section contains activities which are suitable for use with the individual chapters of *Managing Performance & Resources Tutorial* from Osborne Books.

MANAGEMENT INFORMATION

1.1 All kinds of information, and management information in particular, must satisfy certain criteria in order to be useful.

List and explain briefly five criteria which should be satisfied by information if it is to be useful.

1.2 Fino Ltd provides a spray-painting service for manufacturers of various products. The work of Fino Ltd consists of three activities: preparation, painting and storage. The following budgeted information is available for Fino Ltd for the next year:

Activity	Cost Driver	Budgeted Cost Pool	Budgeted Demand
Preparation	Minutes	£375,000	750,000 minutes
Painting	Minutes	£960,000	384,000 minutes
Storage	Cubic metres	£510,000	255,000 cubic metres

Required:

(a) Calculate the cost driver rates for each of the three activities of Fino Ltd.

(b) Calculate the budgeted cost per unit of products X and Y, which require the following:

	X	Y
Preparation	8 minutes	12 minutes
Painting	10 minutes	6 minutes
Storage	0.25 cubic m	0.5 cubic m

1.3 Delta Ltd is an engineering firm which manufactures three products, A, B and C. Product C is produced in smaller quantities for one specific customer. The following planned and budgeted information is available for the coming year:

Overheads:	£
Production set-up costs	246,000
Raw materials inwards department	66,300
Raw materials stores	99,000
Total	411,300

Product:	A	B	C
Budgeted production (units)	40,000	30,000	15,000
Batch size (units)	2,500	3,000	1,000
Direct material cost per unit	£25	£30	£16
Direct labour cost per unit	£4	£2	£1
Direct labour hours per unit	0.5	0.25	0.125
Expected number of raw materials deliveries in year	10	6	10
Expected number of materials requisitions	16	20	30

Required: giving your answers in £ correct to 2 decimal places:

(a)   Calculate a single overhead absorption rate for the total overheads of £411,300 on a direct labour hour basis. (Hint: you will first need to calculate the total labour hours required for the budgeted production of the products.)

(b)   Calculate the direct cost per unit and the total cost per unit of each of the products A, B and C, using absorption costing. Use your answer to (a) to calculate the absorbed overheads.

(c)   In order to apply the Activity Based Costing method to Delta Ltd, a cost driver rate must be calculated for each activity using:

$$\text{Cost driver rate} = \frac{\textit{Budgeted cost pool}}{\textit{Total budgeted demand for cost driver}}$$

Using this method, calculate the cost driver rates to be charged for the three activities as follows:

- Production set-up costs to be charged on the basis of number of batches.
- Raw materials inwards to be charged on the basis of number of deliveries.
- Raw materials stores to be charged on the basis of number of requisitions.

(d)   Using your answers to (c) and Activity Based Costing, calculate the overheads to be included in the total cost of production for each of the products A, B and C.

(e)   Using your answers to (d), calculate the total cost per unit of each of the products A, B and C, using Activity Based Costing. Show the direct cost as a subtotal before adding the overheads in each case.

1.4   Abmar Ltd manufactures one product of the same name, the Abmar. The variable costs of producing 10,000 Abmars during the year ended 30 June 2004 were:

Direct Materials	£70,000
Direct Labour	£40,000
Variable Production Overheads	£30,000

The fixed costs incurred by Abmar Ltd in the year ended 30 June 2004 were:

Fixed production overheads	£50,000
Other fixed overheads	£60,000

The selling price was £30 per Abmar.

Of the 10,000 Abmars produced, only 8,000 were sold during the year.

The opening stock of finished Abmars was zero and there was no opening or closing work-in-progress.

Required:

(a)   Calculate the cost of one Abmar using Marginal Costing.

(b)   Set out a marginal costing statement for Abmar Ltd for the year ended 30 June 2004, showing the contribution (in total) and the total reported profit.

(c)   Given that Fixed Production Overheads are to be absorbed on a per unit basis, but Other Fixed Overheads are not absorbed, calculate the absorption cost of one Abmar.

(d)   Set out an absorption costing statement for Abmar Ltd for the year ended 30 June 2004, showing the total reported profit.

(e)   Calculate the difference in reported profit between your answer in (b) and your answer in (d). What is the reason for this difference?

1.5   The standard cost per unit of a product is as follows:

	£
Direct Materials: 5kg at £5 per kg	25
Direct Labour: 5hrs at £8 per hour	40
Variable production overhead:	
5hrs at £3 per direct labour hour	15
Fixed production overhead:	
5hrs at £4 per direct labour hour	20

Budgeted production totals 1,500 units of the product in a given period.

There are other fixed overheads of £50,000 in total for the period.

The selling price of the product is £170 per unit.

Required:

For each of the following two periods, prepare marginal costing and absorption costing operating statements for this product. In each case, reconcile the reported profit figures for the two costing methods.

(a)   In a given period, 1,500 units of the product are made, but only 1,200 are sold. There is no opening stock of finished goods.

(b)   In the next period, with an opening stock of 300 units, 1,000 units are made and 1,200 are sold.

1.6   Arnold Ltd makes a single product, the Arno. On completion of production, 2% of the Arnos are found to be faulty and have to be scrapped. Production workers work independently of each other in making Arnos, and the production manager wants to establish whether certain workers are responsible for most of the faulty Arnos.

Required:

(a)   Identify two advantages of sampling for establishing the reasons for the faulty Arnos.

(b)   Explain briefly what is meant by

   •   true (or simple) random sampling

   •   systematic sampling

   •   stratified sampling

(c)   State which form of sampling would be most appropriate for Arnold Ltd.

1.7   A moving average trend in Sales Volume has been calculated as follows:

Time period:	3	4	5	6	7	8
Moving average trend (000s units)	931.0	942.4	953.3	964.6	975.7	987.0

Required:

(a)   Calculate the average change in the trend per period.

(b)   Forecast the trend in sales volume for each of the time periods 9, 10, 11 and 12, assuming the trend continues.

1.8   (a)   Calculate a *three-point* moving average trend for the data:

   902   890   940   900   905   950

   (b)   Calculate a *five-point* moving average trend for the data:

   74   77   70   75   80   79   82   74   85   90

1.9   Toto Toys has the following quarterly turnover figures for the three years starting 1 July 2004.

Toto Toys: Turnover in £000s

	Quarter 1	Quarter 2	Quarter 3	Quarter 4
2004			482	560
2005	493	528	520	604
2006	530	571	558	642
2007	570	609		

Required:

(a)   Set out the Toto Toys turnover data in a column and calculate a centred four-point moving average trend.

(b)   Using your answer to (a), calculate average additive (absolute) seasonal variations in turnover.

(c)   Assuming that the trend and the pattern of additive seasonal variations continue, calculate forecast turnover figures for Toto Toys for each of quarters 3 and 4 of 2007.

1.10   Spring Ltd sells a range of outdoor clothing, including lightweight showerproof jackets, for which the quarterly sales volumes over a period of three years are shown below.

	Quarter 1	Quarter 2	Quarter 3	Quarter 4
2003	2,530	2,700	2,610	2,480
2004	2,730	2,940	2,850	2,620
2005	2,950	3,100	3,050	2,820

Required:

(a)   Set out the Spring Ltd data in a column and calculate centred four-point moving average sales volumes for the showerproof jackets. (Use 1 decimal place in workings.)

(b)   Using your answer to (a), calculate average *percentage* seasonal variations (to the nearest whole number) in the sales of Spring Ltd's showerproof jackets.

(c)   Assuming that the trend and the pattern of percentage seasonal variations will continue, forecast the sales volume of Spring Ltd's showerproof jackets for each of the four quarters of 2006.

1.11   An assistant management accountant in Snap Ltd is testing computer software for the analysis of trends and seasonal variations. After inputting several years' historical sales data relating to Snap Ltd's photographic film, the following output has been obtained:

Analysis of sales of photographic film (sales volume in numbers of films)

Regression line trend: $y = 8,000x + 150,000$

This may be written: Trend value = (8,000 x Quarter Number) + 150,000

	Seasonal Variations	
Quarter of the year	*Absolute*	*Percentage*
First	−100,000	−30%
Second	+50,000	+15%
Third	+170,000	+60%
Fourth	−120,000	−45%

Actual numbers of films sold in quarters 17 to 20 are shown below. Quarter 17 was a 'first' quarter of a year, quarter 18 a 'second' quarter, and so on.

Quarter	*Number of films sold*
17	185,000
18	345,500
19	471,600
20	189,000

Required:

(a)   Using the regression line formula, calculate the trend for the sales of films in quarters 17, 18, 19 and 20.

(b)   Using your answer to (a) and the absolute seasonal variations, calculate the resulting forecasts for the film sales in quarters 17 to 20 inclusive.

(c)   Using your answer to (a) and the percentage seasonal variations, calculate the resulting forecasts for the film sales in quarters 17 to 20 inclusive.

(d)   By comparing the two sets of forecasts with the actual film sales given for quarters 17 to 20, identify which method of calculating the seasonal variations gives the best estimates of actual sales of films.

(e)   Using the method which you have identified as best in (d), calculate the forecast sales numbers of films for Snap Ltd for Quarters 21 to 24 inclusive.

1.12   **Required:** answer the following questions using index numbers:

(a)   In the base year of a suitable price index (ie when the index number was 100), product P cost £3. The price index is now 130. What would the cost of product P be in today's terms?

(b)   The market value of a house at the present time is £180,000. A suitable index for house prices is now at a level of 145. What would the price of this house be in terms of the prices 5 years ago, when this house price index was 116?

(c)   A group of workers has been awarded a 2% wage increase for the next year. If the retail prices index goes up from 124 to 128 for the next year, are the workers better or worse off in real terms?

(d)   Average salaries for staff in the head office of a company over 5 years are given below, together with an index of general prices for the same years.

Year	Average Salary	Price Index
1	£16,000	120
2	£16,300	122
3	£16,700	123
4	£17,000	126
5	£17,200	128

•   Calculate the average salaries for each of the five years in terms of Year 5 prices. Give your answers to the nearest £.

•   Comment on the results of your calculations.

(e)   The price of a material is currently £24.00 per kg and a suitable price index is 120. The index is forecast to rise to 125 in a year's time. What would be the forecast price of the material at that time?

After a year, it was found that the index actually rose to 122. Calculate the error in the forecast of the material price.

2 STANDARD COSTING – DIRECT COSTS

2.1   (a)   The standard cost per unit of product A includes:

Direct Material: 2 kg at £5.50 per kg.

In a given period, 10,500 units of product A were made, using 20,000 kg of Direct Material, at a total cost of £98,000.

Required:

Calculate the Direct Material Price and Usage Variances for Product A for this period.

     (b)   The standard cost budget for 1,500 units of product B includes 4,500 metres of Direct Material at a total cost of £5,400.

In a given period, 1,700 units of product B were made, using 5,400 metres of Direct Material, at a total cost of £8,000.

Required:

Calculate the Direct Material Price and Usage Variances for Product B for this period.

2.2   (a)   The standard cost per unit of product A includes:

Direct Labour: 0.5 hours at £6 per hour.

In a given period, 10,500 units of product A were made, taking 5,700 Direct Labour hours, at a total cost of £35,000.

Required:

Calculate the Direct Labour Rate and Efficiency Variances for Product A for this period.

     (b)   The standard cost budget for 1,500 units of product B includes 3,000 hours of Direct Labour at a total cost of £24,000.

In a given period, 1,700 units of product B were made, taking 3,500 Direct Labour hours, at a total cost of £26,000.

Required:

Calculate the Direct Labour Rate and Efficiency Variances For Product B for this period.

2.3   The standard cost per unit of product C includes the following direct costs:

Direct Material: 1.5 kg at £16 per kg = £24 per product unit

Direct Labour: 4 hours at £7 per hour = £28 per product unit

In a given period, the actual results were as follows:

6,300 units of product C were made

10,000 kg of Direct Material were used, total cost £165,400

Direct Labour cost £180,000 for 25,200 hours

Required: for Product C for this period:

(a)   calculate the Direct Material Price and Usage Variances for this period.

(b)   calculate the Direct Labour Rate and Efficiency Variances for this period.

(c)   suggest possible reasons for the direct cost variances in this period.

2.4   State whether each of the following statements is true or false.

(a)   Normal amounts of wastage of direct materials are allowed for when the standard cost of a product is set.

(b)   If more product units are produced than planned, the direct materials usage variance will be adverse.

(c)   If the direct labour (total) variance is adverse, it means that the labour force worked more slowly than the standard.

(d)   Direct materials usage variances are based on the standard prices of the materials.

(e)   If forecasts under-estimate the rate of inflation when standards are set, all the direct cost variances will be adverse.

(f)   Purchasing a substitute for the normal direct material can affect both the price and usage variances.

2.5   The standard cost per unit of a product includes:

  Direct material: 2.5 kg at £9.00 per kg

  Direct Labour: 20 minutes at £6.00 per hour.

In a given period, the actual results were as follows:

  7,620 product units were manufactured.

  Direct material cost £8.80 per kg and 20,000 kg were used.

  Direct labour rate was £6.60 per hour and the total cost was £16,500.

Required:

(a)   Calculate the direct material price and usage variances for the given period.

(b)   Calculate the direct labour rate and efficiency variances for the given period.

(c)   Set out a reconciliation of the standard direct cost of the actual output with the total actual direct cost, showing the variances calculated in (a) and (b).

2.6   Varan Ltd has the following budgeted and actual direct cost and production data for its single product for the last three months.

	Budget	Budget	Actual	Actual
Production units	12,000		12,300	
Direct materials	36,000 m	£223,200	37,000 m	£250,000
Direct labour	24,000 hrs	£115,200	25,000 hrs	£122,500
Total direct costs		£338,400		£372,500

Required: Calculate all the direct cost variances for Varan Ltd for the last three month period and use them to reconcile the standard direct cost for the actual production level with the actual costs.

2.7   Margan Ltd uses marginal costing and has the following budgeted and actual variable cost and production data for the month of November.

	Budget	Budget	Actual	Actual
Production units	8,500		8,200	
Variable materials	10,625 kg	£63,750	10,100 kg	£63,630
Variable labour:				
Grade I	4,250 hrs	£35,700	4,000 hrs	£34,000
Grade II	6,375 hrs	£51,000	6,300 hrs	£50,400
Total variable costs		£150,450		£148,030

Required: Calculate all the relevant variable cost variances (keeping Grade I and II labour separate) and use them to reconcile the standard marginal cost for the actual production level with the actual marginal cost.

2.8   Rust Ltd manufactures a single product, the Rek. The standard direct costs of one Rek are as follows:

Direct Material: 4 kg @ £0.80 per kg =	£3.20
Direct Labour: 1.5 hours @ £8.00 per hour =	£12.00
Total direct cost	£15.20

In October 2004, Rust Ltd produced 9,000 Reks, and the total actual direct costs of production were £30,000 for direct material and £105,000 for direct labour.

The direct material usage variance for October 2004 has been calculated as £800 Favourable, and the Direct Labour Efficiency Variance as £4,000 Adverse.

Required:

(a)   Calculate the total standard direct cost of production for 9,000 Reks.

(b)   Calculate the total actual cost of production for October 2004.

(c)   Calculate the direct material (total) variance for October 2004 and hence calculate the direct material price variance.

(d)   Calculate the direct labour (total) variance for October 2004 and hence calculate the direct labour rate variance.

(e)   Prepare a direct cost reconciliation statement for Rust Ltd for October 2004, showing the total standard and actual costs and all the variances.

(f)   Eight possible separate causes of variances are given below. For each one, state whether it appears to be a valid reason for the variances shown in (e), and if so, to which variances it may have contributed.

   1   Production was interrupted due to a machine breakdown.

2   The supplier has improved the specification of the material.

3   An employee's mistake caused materials to be wasted.

4   There was a national wage increase, applicable to Rust Ltd's employees, which came into force on 1 October 2004.

5   The direct workers included a considerable number of trainees, who started work this month.

6   A bonus was offered to direct workers to encourage greater efficiency.

7   The purchasing department ordered the material from a different supplier.

8   The employees were deliberately working slowly in October to highlight their claim for a pay increase.

2.9   Garth Ltd uses standard costing in the preparation of its budgets. The following information relates to the budgeted and actual results for a given year for product Zed, which is one of the products manufactured by Garth Ltd.

Budget information: Product Zed

Production volume	1,200 units of Zed
Direct material quantity	7,200 kg
Total cost of direct material	£36,000
Direct labour hours	8,400 hours
Total direct labour cost	£50,400

Actual results : Product Zed

Production volume	1,400 units of Zed
Direct material quantity	8,200 kg
Total cost of direct material	£42,640
Direct labour hours	9,400 hours
Total direct labour cost	£56,500

During this period, a customer put in an extra order for Product Zed at short notice, which meant that a batch of direct material had to be purchased from a local supplier. This material was slightly different from that normally used in Product Zed, and was more expensive. Some overtime was worked to complete the order on time and the premium paid to employees for this was included in the direct labour cost.

Required:

(a)   Calculate all the direct material and direct labour variances for Product Zed for the given year.

(b)   Prepare a statement reconciling the standard direct cost of actual output with the actual direct cost of Product Zed for the given year.

(c)   Write a Memo to the manager of Garth Ltd, suggesting reasons for the difference between the standard and actual costs.

3 STANDARD COSTING – FIXED OVERHEADS

3.1 The budget for product A for a given period includes £48,000 of fixed overheads, to be absorbed on direct labour hours at a rate of £8 per direct labour hour. The planned production of product A is 12,000 units, the standard direct labour hours being 0.5 hours per unit of product A.

The actual results for the period were as follows:

10,500 units of product A were made, taking 5,700 direct labour hours.

Total actual fixed overheads amounted to £50,000.

Required:

Calculate for product A for the given period:

- the total fixed overhead variance

- the fixed overhead expenditure variance

- the fixed overhead volume variance

- the fixed overhead capacity variance

- the fixed overhead efficiency variance

3.2 The planned production of product B for a given period is 1,500 units. The standard cost per unit of B includes fixed overheads absorbed at a rate of £30 per direct labour hour. Each unit of B should take 2 hours of direct labour according to the standard.

In the given period, 1,700 units of product B were actually made, taking 3,500 direct labour hours. The actual fixed overheads were £85,000.

Required:

Calculate for product B for the given period:

- the total fixed overhead variance

- the fixed overhead expenditure variance

- the fixed overhead volume variance

- the fixed overhead capacity variance

- the fixed overhead efficiency variance

3.3 Margan Ltd uses marginal costing and has the following budgeted and actual fixed cost data for the month of November.

	Budget	Actual
Production units	8,500	8,200
Fixed costs	£90,100	£85,000

Required:

(a)   Calculate the fixed cost (expenditure) variance for Margan Ltd for November.

(b)   Explain briefly why there is no further analysis of fixed cost variances when marginal costing is being used.

3.4   The standard direct labour time per unit of a product is 20 minutes. Fixed overheads are to be absorbed on direct labour hours at an overhead absorption rate of £12.60 per hour, based on budgeted production of 7,800 units.

In a given period, the actual results were as follows:

7,620 product units were manufactured.

Direct labour hours used were 2,500 hours.

Actual fixed production overhead amounted to £33,000.

Required:

(a)   Calculate the following fixed overhead variances for this product for the given period:
- total fixed overhead variance
- fixed overhead expenditure variance
- fixed overhead capacity variance
- fixed overhead efficiency variance
- fixed overhead volume variance

(b)   Which of the following statements is true for this case?

1   Production output was more than planned, resulting in a favourable efficiency variance.

2   Direct labour hours were less than planned, resulting in an adverse capacity variance.

3   Fixed overheads were over-absorbed.

4   Output was produced using less hours than the standard for the actual number of units.

5   Spending on fixed overheads was less than expected.

3.5   Varan Ltd has the following budgeted and actual direct cost and production data for its single product for the last three months.

	Budget	Budget	Actual	Actual
Production units	12,000		12,300	
Direct materials	36,000 m	£223,200	37,000 m	£250,000
Direct labour	24,000 hrs	£115,200	25,000 hrs	£122,500
Fixed production overhead		£14,400		£16,000
Machine hours	18,000 hrs		18,500 hrs	

Required:

(a)   Calculate the fixed production overhead absorption rate for Varan Ltd, based on machine hours.

(b)   Calculate the budgeted amount of fixed production overhead per unit of the product, using your answer to (a).

(c)   Calculate all the direct cost variances for Varan Ltd for the last three month period. (You may have already calculated these in Activity 2.6.)

(d)   Calculate all the fixed overhead variances for Varan Ltd for the last three month period.

(e)   Prepare a reconciliation statement for Varan Ltd's actual output for the last three months, showing the total standard and actual costs and all the variances calculated in (c) and (d) above.

(f)   Seven possible separate causes of variances are given below. For each one, state whether it appears to be a valid reason for the variances shown in (e), and if so, to which variances it may have contributed.

1   A customer increased his order for the product at short notice.

2   Due to extra demand for the product, insufficient direct materials were in stock, and a slightly different substitute material had to be obtained at short notice from a different supplier.

3   Production was interrupted due to a machine breakdown.

4   There was a national wage increase, applicable to Varan Ltd's employees, which came into force during this period.

5   A number of production staff were off sick and therefore additional overtime was worked by others.

6   A bonus was offered to direct workers to encourage greater efficiency.

7   There have been improvements in production methods since the standard was set.

3.6   Island Holidays Ltd specialises in arranging holidays to a small island. The company uses its own 105-seat aircraft to transfer tourists to and from the island. The following report was presented to the manager of Island Holidays Ltd:

Island Holidays Ltd Operating Statement for Quarter 3, 2004

	Budget	Actual
Number of holidays	6,000	7,800
	£	£
Turnover	1,800,000	2,262,000
Accommodation	840,000	1,048,944
Air transport	720,000	792,000
Operating profit	240,000	421,056

The manager considers this report unhelpful and requests a standard costing report, reconciling the standard and actual costs for the actual holidays sold in the quarter. You are given the following additional information:

The accommodation cost is a variable cost and the usage variance is zero.

Air transport is a fixed cost.

The budget for a volume of 6,000 holidays was based on air transport capacity of 80 return flights in the quarter, with an average of 75 tourists per flight. These standards were used to calculate the fixed overhead absorption rate when costing individual holidays.

Due to weather conditions, there were only 78 flights in this quarter, carrying a total of 7,800 tourists.

Required:

(a)   Using the budgeted data, calculate the standard absorption cost per holiday

(b)   Using your answer to (a), calculate the standard absorption cost of 7,800 holidays

(c)   Calculate the following variances:

  •   material price variance for accommodation

  •   fixed overhead expenditure variance for air transport

  •   fixed overhead volume variance for air transport

  •   fixed overhead capacity variance for air transport

  •   fixed overhead efficiency variance for air transport

(d)   Prepare a statement reconciling the standard absorption cost of 7,800 holidays to the actual total cost of 7,800 holidays

(e)   Calculate the actual total cost per holiday and identify the most important reason why this was lower than the standard absorption cost per holiday.

3.7   Image Dry Cleaners run four shops, each of which is equipped with a dry cleaning machine. Whenever possible, each machine is run with a full load, which is on average 20 items. The shops are open six days a week, and each machine can be used to dry clean a maximum of 5 loads per day, but Image's budget is set on the basis of 4 loads per machine per weekday, and 2 loads per machine on Saturdays. Image Dry Cleaners' budgeted fixed overheads are £6,160 per week and are absorbed on a machine run basis, with the standard set at an average load of 15 items per machine run.

During the week commencing 10 September 2004, the actual fixed overheads amounted to £6,010. Results from the Image shops showed:

	Number of machine runs	Items cleaned
North shop	18	288
South shop	24	384
East shop	20	300
West shop	20	288
Total	82	1,260

Required:

(a)   Identify the output of Image Dry Cleaners and how it is measured in standard form. Calculate the fixed overhead absorption rate per machine run.

(b)   Calculate all the fixed overhead variances for Image Dry Cleaners for the week commencing 10 September 2004.

(c)   Write a short report to the manager of Image Dry Cleaners, summarising the subdivision of the fixed overhead variance into expenditure, volume, capacity and efficiency variances. Include brief comments on the meaning of these variances in relation to the actual results and the usefulness of the analysis.

3.8   The Village Museum is a small private museum, which is open each day except Monday, throughout the year. The costs of running the museum are all costs which relate to time periods and do not depend on the number of visitors. Visitors are charged for entry and can stay as long as they wish in the museum on that day. The fixed costs for the first six months of the current year were budgeted as £8,400 and the total number of visitors expected was 2,400.

The actual fixed costs for the first six months of the current year were £8,670 and the actual total number of visitors was 2,550.

Required:

(a)   Calculate a fixed cost absorption rate for the museum, based on the number of visitors.

(b)   Calculate the fixed cost variance for the first six months of the current year, and analyse it into expenditure and volume variances. State why each of these variances has arisen.

(c)   Explain briefly why analysis of the volume variance into capacity and efficiency variances would not be relevant in this case.

3.9   The Riviera Swimming Pool is open for 1,200 hours per quarter. There should be five staff on duty throughout opening hours. The cost budget for the second quarter of 2004 is shown below, together with the actual costs for the quarter.

Riviera Swimming Pool: Quarter 2, 2004

	Budget	*Actual*
Opening hours	1,200	1,200
Direct material for water treatment: quantity (litres)	4,500	4,620
Direct material cost (£)	8,100	8,300
Direct labour hours	6,000	5,900
Direct labour cost (£)	32,400	32,450
Fixed overheads (£)	28,000	30,000
Number of customer visits	20,000	18,600

Required:

(a)   Calculate:

- the standard cost per litre of direct material

- the standard cost per direct labour hour

- the fixed overhead absorption rate, based on the number of customer visits

(b)   Calculate, for quarter 2, 2004:

- the direct material price variance

- the direct labour rate variance

- the fixed overhead expenditure variance

- the fixed overhead volume variance, based on the budgeted and actual numbers of customer visits

(c)   Explain briefly why it is not appropriate to split the fixed overhead volume variance into capacity and efficiency variances in this case.

4 STANDARD COSTING – FURTHER ANALYSIS

4.1 (a)   Explain briefly the meaning and implications of each of the following, in relation to standard costing:

- ideal standard
- attainable standard
- basic standard

Which of these is most appropriate for the purposes of variance analysis and why?

(b)   Explain briefly what is meant by the following terms in relation to variance analysis:

- control limits
- management by exception

(c)   Give one example of how methods of costing and the setting of standards may affect the behaviour of a manager who is held responsible for particular variances.

4.2   The standard cost per litre of a material is £3.20, based on its expected average price over the coming year. Time series analysis of the cost of this item over the last 5 years indicates that the following additive seasonal variations in the price can be expected.

Quarter 1	January to March	– £0.10
2	April to June	+ £0.05
3	July to September	+ £0.10
4	October to December	– £0.05

Required:

Using the given data for each of the following months, calculate the Material Price Variance for this material, and analyse it into the part expected to be due to the seasonality of the price and the part due to other influences.

(a)   In January, 18,000 litres were used, at a total cost of £54,000.

(b)   In May, 18,000 litres were used, at a total cost of £58,140.

4.3   The standard cost per metre of a material is £20, based on its expected average price over the coming year. Time series analysis of the cost of this item over the last 5 years indicates that the following proportional (multiplicative) seasonal variations in the price can be expected.

Quarter 1	January to March	+15%
2	April to June	+5%
3	July to September	– 20%
4	October to December	zero

Required:

Using the given data for each of the following months, calculate the Material Price Variance for this material, and analyse it into the part expected to be due to the seasonality of the price and the part due to other influences.

(a)   In May, 6,400 metres were used, at a total cost of £124,800.

(b)   In September, 7,000 metres were used, at a total cost of £105,000.

4.4   A business set its standard price for a certain material when the appropriate price index was 148. The assumption was made that the index would rise to 150 by the time the standard was in use, and therefore the standard decided upon was £60 per unit of material, to take this into account. By the time the standard was in use, the index had actually risen to 152 and in a given month 5,800 units of material actually cost £350,900.

Required:

Calculate the Material Price Variance for this material, and analyse it into the part due to the actual change in the price index and the part due to other factors.

4.5   When standards were being decided upon, the appropriate wage rate index was expected to rise from 180 to 189, and the standard wage rate was set as £7.35 per hour to take account of this. In fact, by the time the standard was in use, an increase of 4% had been brought in for the relevant employees. In a given period, £79,056 was paid for a total of 10,800 hours.

Required:

Calculate the Labour Rate Variance for this period, and analyse it into the part due to the actual pay award and the part due to other factors.

4.6   A company imports a direct material from Beta Island and pays in Beta Dollars (B$). The standard price per unit of the material was set in B$, equivalent to £36, when the exchange rate was B$5 to the £. The exchange rate is subject to fluctuations, however, due to instability in the Beta Island economy.

Required:

For each of the following months, calculate the Material Price Variance, and analyse it into the part due to exchange rate changes and the part due to other factors.

(a)   In June the exchange rate was B$4.50 = £1. In June 7,500 units of material cost £307,500 in total.

(b)   In September the exchange rate was B$6 = £1. In September 8,000 units of material cost £256,000 in total.

4.7   A company imports a direct material from Gamma Island and pays in Gamma Dollars (G$). The standard price per unit of the material was set in G$, equivalent to £40, when the exchange rate was G$30 to the £. The exchange rate is subject to fluctuations, however, due to instability in the Gamma Island economy.

Required:

For each of the following months, calculate the Material Price Variance, and analyse it into the part due to exchange rate changes and the part due to other factors.

(a)   In July the exchange rate was G$32 = £1. In July 4,800 units of material cost £168,000 in total.

(b)   In November the exchange rate was G$25 = £1. In November 5,200 units of material cost £260,000 in total.

4.8   The standard cost per unit of product UV includes:

Direct material: 4 kg at £2.50 per kg, ie £10.00 per unit of UV

Direct Labour: 1.5 hours at £6.20 per hour, ie £9.30 per unit of UV

In a given period, the actual results were that 4,500 units of UV were produced, using 20,000 kg of direct material and taking 6,400 direct labour hours. The total cost of direct material was £48,000 and the total cost of direct labour was £40,000.

Required: for Product UV for the given period:

(a)   calculate the direct material total variance and split it into price and usage variances.

(b)   calculate the direct labour total variance and split it into rate and efficiency variances.

(c)   After calculating the variances as above, additional information becomes available:

The standard for direct material usage should have been changed to 4.2 kg per unit of UV for this period, due to a change in its specification.

The standard for direct labour time was set at 90% level of efficiency for a previous period, when staff were being trained. For the given period, 100% level of efficiency was expected and the standard had not been updated.

(i)   Calculate the part of the direct material usage variance due to the incorrect standard and the part due to other reasons.

(ii)   Calculate the part of the direct labour efficiency variance due to the out of date level of efficiency in the standard and the part due to other reasons.

4.9   The standard cost per unit of product W includes:

Direct material: 7 kg at £8.00 per kg, ie £56.00 per unit of W

Direct Labour: 4 hours at £5.00 per hour, ie £20.00 per unit of W

In a given period, the actual results were that 16,000 units of W were produced, using 113,600 kg of direct material and taking 68,640 direct labour hours. The total cost of direct material was £920,160 and the total cost of direct labour was £336,336.

Required: for Product W for the given period:

(a)   calculate the direct material total variance and split it into price and usage variances.

(b)   calculate the direct labour total variance and split it into rate and efficiency variances.

(c)   After calculating the variances as above, additional information becomes available:

The standard for the price of direct material should have been increased by 1.25% for this period, due to a change in supplier.

Production workers are new to this work and are currently taking 10% longer to make a unit of W than they will when fully trained.

(i)   Calculate the part of the direct material price variance due to the incorrect standard and the part due to other reasons.

(ii)   Calculate the part of the direct labour efficiency variance due to the production workers not yet being fully trained and the part due to other reasons.

4.10 Brighter Chemicals makes a single product, XZ, which is sold in 5-litre tins. Fixed overheads are absorbed on the basis of direct labour hours. Budgeted production is 1,750 tins per month and the standard cost per tin is as follows:

Direct material: 5 litres at £40 per litre = £200 per tin of XZ

Direct labour: 10 hours at £6 per hour = £60 per tin of XZ

Fixed overheads: 10 hours at £24 per hour = £240 per tin of XZ

During the month of May 2004, actual production was 1,700 tins of XZ and the actual total costs were as follows:

Direct material	£338,283
Direct labour	£110,330
Fixed overheads	£410,000

The actual cost of direct material was £40.20 per litre and the actual direct labour rate was £5.90 per hour.

Required:

(a) Calculate for the month of May 2004:

    (i) actual litres of material used

    (ii) actual hours worked

    (iii) standard quantity of material for the actual output of 1,700 tins of XZ

    (iv) standard direct labour hours for the actual output of 1,700 tins of XZ

    (v) the total budgeted fixed overheads

(b) Calculate the following variances for the month of May 2004:

    (i) direct material price variance

    (ii) direct material usage variance

    (iii) direct labour rate variance

    (iv) direct labour efficiency variance

    (v) fixed overhead expenditure variance

    (vi) fixed overhead volume variance

    (vii) fixed overhead capacity variance

    (viii) fixed overhead efficiency variance

(c) Prepare a statement for the month of May 2004, reconciling the standard cost of the actual output of XZ to the actual cost, detailing the variances

(d)   You are given the following additional information after preparing the statement in part (c):

- the direct material used is purchased in drums, each of which has a guaranteed minimum content

- the tins of output of XZ are filled by a machine and the amounts put into the tins may vary very slightly

- an appropriate index of raw material prices was 124.00 when the direct material standard price was set, but by May 2004 it was actually 125.86

You are asked to write a short memo to the production director, explaining:

(i)   three factors which may have contributed to the favourable direct material usage variance, but which do not represent efficient usage of the material

(ii)   why it is important to investigate favourable variances as well as adverse variances

(iii) how the material price variance has arisen partly due to the change in the standard cost as measured by the material price index and partly due to other reasons, showing your calculation of these two parts.

5 MEASURING QUALITY

5.1 The managers of a large department store wish to review the quality of the *service* (not the products) provided to customers in the various store departments. They have decided to carry out a survey, by asking customers to complete a short questionnaire.

Required:

(a) Suggest four aspects of the service that should be covered by the questionnaire.

(b) For each of the four categories listed below, give an example of a cost of quality of the service offered by the department store.

- Prevention costs

- Appraisal costs

- Internal failure costs

- External failure costs

5.2 (a) Explain briefly the implications and the benefits of implementing a policy of Total Quality Management in an organisation.

(b) Suggest how an organisation with a policy of Total Quality Management may tackle the following problems:

- A large number of complaints from customers that they are unable to get through on the telephone when they wish to place an order.

- Several cases of materials being wasted due to machine failure.

5.3 Smith's Wheels make wheels for model trains. The wheels are made by automatic machining and then assembled in pairs on axles. The wheels are sold to individual model-makers, model railway clubs, shops and to toy manufacturers to incorporate in their model trains. Accurate machining and assembly of the wheels and axles is essential for the trains to work.

After the machining process 2% of the wheels are scrapped because they are faulty. It is estimated that, after assembly, 4% of the finished products are substandard and Smith's inspection identifies three-quarters of these, which are also scrapped.

Smith's Wheels guarantee to replace any faulty wheels returned by customers.

The variable cost of making each wheel is £0.20 and the cost of the axle and assembly for each pair is £0.15, so that the variable cost of the finished product is £0.55.

In a given period, Smith's Wheels commence production with machining 40,000 wheels. Assume that all finished production which passes inspection is sold, and all faulty wheels sold are returned.

Required: for the given period:

(a)   Calculate the number of wheels scrapped after machining.

(b)   Calculate the number of substandard assembled pairs of wheels, and the quantity of these which are scrapped. How many substandard products are therefore sold?

(c)   Calculate the costs of quality associated with your answers to (a) and (b) above.

(d)   Identify two further costs of quality for Smith's Wheels which are not included in your calculations.

5.4   White Ltd runs a linen supply service for a number of hotels in a large city. Clean towels, sheets etc, supplied from White Ltd's own stock, are delivered to each hotel on a daily basis. Used linen is collected and laundered in White Ltd's own laundry.

Problems arise with the hotels if delivery is delayed, if the standard of cleanliness or the condition of items is unsatisfactory, or if the numbers of items supplied is incorrect. There have recently been a number of complaints from hotel managers about the service offered by White Ltd.

The managing director of White Ltd held a meeting with staff representatives from all departments, whose comments included the following:

*   The laundry has recently started using cheaper washing liquid.

*   The delivery vans have broken down three times in three months.

*   The requirements from the hotels come in by telephone. The calls are often made by a junior employee at the hotel and may contain mistakes. A junior White Ltd employee may take the calls.

*   Delivery routes have not been reviewed for over a year, during which time several new hotels have been added and some new road traffic schemes have been introduced in the city.

*   Some of the equipment in the laundry is out-dated and inefficient.

*   Packing staff do not have sufficient time to inspect the items thoroughly or to double check the count of items in the bags.

Required: for White Ltd's linen supply service:

(a)   Identify the features of the service which represent its value to the customer.

(b)   Suggest ways in which the problems identified at the meeting may be addressed, and the associated effects on costs of quality which would arise in each case.

5.5   Pix Ltd manufactures cameras, and has recently carried out an investigation into the reliability of one of its relatively new products, a digital camera. Investigations show that 1 in every 1,500 of these cameras quickly develops a fault and ceases to work. It is estimated that 80% of these are returned to Pix Ltd. A repair which costs the company £30 corrects the fault.

A further 2 in every 1,500 of these cameras are returned to Pix Ltd because they are considered by customers to produce unsatisfactory results. Pix Ltd gives these customers full refunds, and after checking the cameras at a cost of £10, sells them as 'reconditioned' at a discount of £100 on the usual selling price.

It is estimated that the costs of advertising in order to replace customers who were dissatisfied with Pix Ltd's digital cameras amount to £60,000 per year. Average sales of these digital cameras are currently 75,000 per year, but Pix Ltd's managers had anticipated significant sales growth in the coming year.

Required:

List the explicit costs of quality in this case, stating the category of each and the amount where possible.

Identify an example of an implicit cost of quality in this case.

5.6   (a)   From your own point of view as a consumer, suggest the features which give a camera its value.

(b)   From the point of view of a camera manufacturer, list four questions which may be asked in carrying out a value analysis of their products.

5.7   **Required:**

(a)   Give two reasons why it is important to plan long-term cost reduction policies, rather than introduce crash programmes for cutting costs.

(b)   Suggest two ways in which work study may help to reduce costs in a factory.

(c)   List three ways in which a manufacturing company may reduce costs, other than on production.

(d)   'Value engineering' may be applied to a new product being developed. What are the main implications this would have for the design of the product?

(e)   Explain briefly what is meant by the statement 'variety reduction can reduce costs and enhance value'.

5.8   Gill Ltd make a single product, the Gamma, each unit of which uses a component G3. Purchases of G3 are all inspected on receipt and some are found to be faulty. These are returned to the supplier, but further units of G3 develop faults when used in the product Gamma. As a result, costs are incurred in reworking production and in dealing with complaints in customer services.

In the following operating statement for Gill Ltd, marginal costing is used. Gill Ltd keeps no stocks of materials other than G3, nor of finished Gammas.

Gill Ltd: Operating Statement for the year ended 31 December 2004

	£000s	£000s
Turnover		1,800
Purchases of G3	350	
Less: returns of G3	(30)	
	320	
Add: opening stock	40	
Less: closing stock	(20)	
G3 issued to production	340	
Other variable costs	400	740
Contribution		1,060
Fixed production overhead	810	
G3 inspection costs	22	
Costs relating to purchases returns	12	
Costs of reworking	30	
Customer services relating to G3 faults	43	
Administration	25	
Selling and distribution	35	977
Net operating profit		83

The directors of Gill Ltd are concerned about the high cost of quality relating to G3. Guaranteed fault-free supplies of G3 could be obtained from the supplier at a 15% higher purchase price per unit.

Required:

(a)   Explain what is meant by 'explicit' costs of quality.

(b)   Identify the explicit costs of quality incurred by Gill Ltd in the year ended 31 December 2004.

(c)   Explain what is meant by 'implicit' costs of quality and give one example of such costs for Gill Ltd for the year ended 31 December 2004.

(d)   Advise the directors of Gill Ltd as to whether the fault-free supplies of G3 at the higher price would be worthwhile.

5.9   The managers of Lodden plc have decided to launch a new product, XL, at a selling price of £375 per unit. Market research suggests that sales of 18,000 units of XL should be achieved in the next year at this selling price. Lodden plc has a target level of operating profit of 20% on sales for this product.

Required:

(a) Calculate:

   (i) the expected total sales revenue from XL for the next year

   (ii) the target operating profit required by Lodden plc from sales of XL for the next year

   (iii) the total target cost for XL for the next year

   (iv) the target cost per unit of XL

(b) Explain briefly how value engineering may be used by Lodden plc in order to achieve the target cost per unit of XL.

5.10 Nett plc is a manufacturer of computers and related products. The managers of Nett plc are considering developing a processor for a number of specialised applications. The processor would have a relatively short life cycle, for which the following forecasts have been made:

- research, development and design would cost £60,000

- sales would take place over the following 3 years

- production costs would be £120,000 per year for 3 years plus £50 per unit

- selling and distribution costs would be £80,000 per year for 3 years plus £40 per unit

- customer support would cost £95,000 per year for 3 years and £75,000 per year for a further 2 years

- the total sales demand for the processor over the whole of its life cycle has been estimated at two possible prices:

   Case 1:   5,000 units at £400 per unit

   Case 2:   4,500 units at £480 per unit

Required:

(a) Calculate for each of the two possible selling prices per unit:

   (i) the total life cycle sales revenue from the processor

   (ii) the total life cycle costs of the processor (assuming production and sales volumes are equal)

   (iii) the total life cycle profit from the processor

(b) Make a recommendation to the managers of Nett plc regarding the processor, given that the company's target level of profit is 30% on sales.

6 MEASURING PERFORMANCE

6.1 (a) What are performance indicators used for?

(b) Why are comparisons more useful than individual figures?

(c) List three kinds of comparisons which are useful.

6.2 The following profit and loss accounts relate to a wholesale trader selling electrical accessories such as cables, switches and so on:

M. Lomas: Profit and Loss Account for the year ended:

	30 June 2004		30 June 2003	
	£000s	£000s	£000s	£000s
Sales		780		675
Less: Cost of Sales				
Opening stock	60		90	
Purchases	520		410	
Less: Closing Stock	(40)	540	(60)	440
Gross Profit		240		235
Less: Expenses:				
Administration	60		45	
Selling	40	100	30	75
Net Profit		140		160

Required:

Calculate the following ratios for M. Lomas for the given years (correct to 1 decimal place):

- gross profit percentage
- net profit percentage
- each expense as a percentage of sales

Comment briefly on the original figures and on the percentages calculated.

6.3 The following are extracts from the financial accounts of Robins Ltd, manufacturers of artificial Christmas trees.

Robins Ltd: Extract from Profit and Loss Account
for the year ended 30 September:

	2004	2003
	£000s	£000s
Turnover	2,000	1,920
Operating Profit	267	240

Balance Sheet extract as at 30 September:

	2004		2003	
	£000s	£000s	£000s	£000s
Fixed assets (Net Book Value)		900		840
Current Assets:	120		110	
Current liabilities	(130)	(10)	(90)	20
Net Assets		890		860
Long-term loans		(50)		–
		840		860

Required:

(a) State the formulae for the following ratios and calculate them for Robins Ltd for the given years, (correct to 2 decimal places):

- return on capital employed
- asset turnover
- operating profit margin

(b) What is the relationship between the three ratios in (a)?

(c) Referring to the relationship between the ratios, identify the reason for the change in the ROCE from the first to second year.

6.4 Craig Ltd is a wholesaler, trading in plastics and specialised paints. Operating statements are given below for Craig Ltd for the years ended 31 December 2003 and 2004, together with balance sheet extracts as at those dates.

Craig Ltd: Operating Statements for the years ended 31 December

	2004		2003	
	£000s	£000s	£000s	£000s
Sales		602		587
Less: Cost of Sales				
Opening stock	14		38	
Purchases	428		375	
Less: closing stock	(20)	422	(14)	399
Gross Profit		180		188
Administration	64		62	
Selling and distribution	46	110	36	98
Operating profit		70		90

Craig Ltd: Balance Sheet Extracts as at 31 December

	2004		2003	
	£000s	£000s	£000s	£000s
Fixed assets at cost		330		300
Accumulated depreciation		(80)		(50)
		250		250
Current assets:				
Stock	20		14	
Debtors	73		58	
Cash at bank	-		12	
	93		84	
Current liabilities:				
Creditors	38		35	
Bank overdraft	2		-	
	40		35	
Net current assets		53		49
Net assets		303		299

Required:

(a) Identify the **two** most significant changes (from 2003 to 2004) in the given data for Craig Ltd

(b) For Craig Ltd for the given years, calculate:

    (i)   gross profit margin on sales

    (ii)   operating profit margin on sales

    (iii)   return on capital employed

    (iv)   asset turnover

    (v)   average age of debtors in days

    (vi)   average age of stock in days (using average stock)

    (vii)   average creditors' payment period in days

    (viii)   current ratio

    (ix)   quick (acid test) ratio

(c) Identify the **two** most significant changes (from 2003 to 2004) in the ratios you have calculated in (b) and comment briefly on possible reasons for these changes.

6.5 Laito Dairies Ltd is a chain of dairies (which process, bottle and distribute milk products) of which Newtown Dairy is one local division. The information below relates to Newtown Dairy.

Newtown Dairy: report for the year ended 31 July 2004

Summary Profit and Loss Account for the year ended 31 July 2004

	£000s	£000s
Turnover		1,300
Less: Cost of Sales		
Opening Stock	2	
Cost of Production	540	
Less: Closing Stock	(4)	538
Gross Profit		762
Administration	250	
Selling and Distribution	360	610
Operating Profit		152

Balance Sheet extract as at 31 July 2004:

	£000s	£000s	£000s
Fixed assets	*Land and Buildings*	*Plant*	*Total*
At cost	800	1,200	2,000
Additions	–	300	300
	800	1,500	2,300
Accumulated depreciation	–	600	600
	800	900	1,700
Current Assets:			
Raw materials stock	3		
Finished goods stock	4		
Debtors	45		
Cash at bank	25		
	77		
Current liabilities	(110)		(33)
Net Assets			1,667

Required (working correct to 1 decimal place):

(a)   Calculate the following ratios for Newtown Dairy for the given year:
- gross profit margin
- operating profit margin
- return on capital employed (ROCE)
- asset turnover
- the average age of debtors
- the average age of finished goods stock (using average stock)

(b)   Stating the formulae you are using, calculate the current and quick (acid test) ratios for Newtown Dairy and identify one feature of the business which has an effect on these ratios in this case.

(c)   The directors of Laito Dairies Ltd consider that ROCE and Asset Turnover are important performance measures, and Newtown Dairy has failed to meet the company targets, which are:

Target ROCE: 15%   Target Asset turnover: 1.2 times

Assuming that the given balance sheet data is unchanged, calculate:

(i)   the amount of Operating Profit which Newtown Dairy would have obtained in the given year if it had achieved the company target level of ROCE

(ii)   the amount of Turnover which Newtown Dairy would have obtained if it had achieved the company target level of Asset Turnover

6.6   A summary of the trading account for Wold Ltd for a given year is as follows:

	£
Sales	285,000
Less: returns	1,200
	283,800
Cost of sales	198,660
Gross profit	85,140

Required:

(a)   Calculate the closing debtors figure for Wold Ltd for the given year if all the sales are on credit and the average age of closing debtors is 1.2 months.

(b)   Calculate the closing stock figure for Wold Ltd for the given year if the average age of closing stock is 2 months.

(c)   Calculate the closing creditors figure for Wold Ltd for the given year if the cost of sales includes £201,760 of credit purchases and the average age of closing creditors is 1.5 months.

6.7   Walkers Ltd operates a chain of retail shoe shops. Walkers Ltd uses common accounting policies in all branches. The method of straight-line depreciation is used for fixed assets, which are mainly fixtures and fittings. The shops are rented, rent being included in 'other costs' below.

Branch managers are responsible for the control of stock and debtors and payments to creditors, but cash received is all paid into the Walkers Ltd bank account the same day.

Financial data relating to the Redridge Branch of Walkers Ltd is shown on the next page.

Walkers Ltd Redridge Branch Year ended 31 March 2004

Operating Statement for the year ended 31 March 2004

	£000s	£000s
Turnover		540.0
Less: Cost of Sales		
Opening Stock	70.0	
Purchases	270.0	
Less Closing Stock	(59.2)	280.8
Gross Profit		259.2
Wages and salaries	135.0	
Depreciation	22.0	
Other costs	45.5	202.5
Operating profit		56.7

Operating net assets as at 31 March 2004

	£000s	£000s
Fixed Assets at cost		220.0
Accumulated depreciation		88.0
Net Book Value		132.0
Working capital:		
Stock	59.2	
Debtors	27.0	
Creditors	(45.0)	41.2
Net assets		173.2

Required:

(a)   For Walkers Ltd Redridge Branch, for the given year, calculate:

- return on capital employed
- gross profit margin as a percentage
- asset turnover
- operating profit margin as a percentage
- the average age of debtors in days

- the average age of creditors in days
- the average age of stock (using closing stock) in days

(b)   The directors of Walkers Ltd have set certain targets which they consider the branches should be able to achieve. These targets are:

ROCE	37.5%
Asset Turnover	3.5 times per year
Average age of debtors	15 days
Average age of creditors	65 days
Average age of closing stock	70 days

(i)   If Redridge Branch had achieved the company target level of Asset Turnover, while maintaining prices and the existing capital employed, what percentage would the ROCE have been?

(ii)   If Redridge Branch had achieved the company targets for the average age of debtors, average age of creditors and average age of closing stock, while maintaining the same turnover and profit, what would the ROCE and the Asset Turnover have been?

(c)   Comment briefly on the results for the Redridge Branch for the given year and its performance in relation to the Walkers Ltd targets. State two limitations of the use of ratios in this way for Walkers Ltd to measure the performance of its branch managers.

6.8   Lime plc is a manufacturer of roofing materials for industrial buildings and its results for the year ended 31 March 2004 are shown below.

Lime plc Summary Profit and Loss Account for the year ended 31 March 2004

	£000s	£000s
Turnover		932
Less: sales returns		(10)
		922
Less: Cost of Sales		
Opening stock	38	
Cost of Production	484	
Less: closing stock	(43)	479
Gross Profit		443
Administration	138	
Selling and distribution	165	303
Operating profit		140

Lime plc Summary Balance Sheet Extract as at 31 March 2004

	£000s	£000s
Fixed assets at cost		815
Accumulated depreciation		272
		543
Current assets:		
Raw materials stock	12	
Finished goods stock	43	
Debtors	150	
Cash	6	
	211	
Current liabilities	(84)	127
		670
Long-term liabilities: debentures		(50)
		620

Required:

(a)   Calculate for Lime plc for the year ended 31 March 2004:

(i)   Gross profit margin

(ii)   Operating profit margin

(iii) Return on capital employed (ROCE)

(iv) Asset turnover

(v)   Average age of finished goods stock (using closing stock) in months

(vi) Debtors' collection period in months

(b)   Comment briefly on the results for Lime plc for the year ended 31 March 2004, given the additional information:

- the normal credit terms allowed to customers by Lime plc state that payment is due within 30 days

- in February 2003, the management of Lime plc had set the following targets for the year ended 31 March 2004:

  Return on capital employed 22.5%

  Operating profit margin 15%

- several machines used in production were replaced by new ones in December 2003. The new machines are more efficient. There is lower demand for Lime plc's products in the Winter, so the replacement work did not affect production.

7 MEASURING PERFORMANCE – FURTHER ASPECTS

7.1 Turnover and net profit figures are given in the following spreadsheet for Ray Ltd for the five years ended 31 December 2009.

Required: Enter suitable spreadsheet formulas in rows 5, 6 and 7, cells B to F. Show separately the results that would be obtained in those cells.

Comment on the results obtained.

	A	B	C	D	E	F
1	Year	2005	2006	2007	2008	2009
2	Turnover (£000s)	358	362	365	366	373
3	Net Profit (£000s)	55	57	59	60	62
4	Industry index	131	134	136	137	140
5	Turnover in 2009 terms (£000s)					
6	Net profit in 2009 terms (£000s)					
7	Net profit percentage in 2009 terms					

7.2 The following information is given for Ray Ltd for the year ended 31 December 2009.

Turnover	£373,000
Number of employees	20
Cost of materials used	£80,000
Total cost of bought-in services	£120,000

Required: calculate the total value added and the value added per employee for the year ended 31 December 2009 for Ray Ltd.

7.3 The following information is given for VAC Ltd for the year ended 31 August 2004.

Turnover	£590,000
Output (product units)	40,000
Number of employees	35
Cost of materials used	£130,000
Total cost of bought-in services	£195,000
Total cost of inputs	£325,000

Required: calculate for VAC Ltd for the year ended 31 August 2004:

- total value added
- value added per employee
- material cost per unit
- total cost of inputs per unit

7.4 For each of the following activities or aspects of work, suggest a suitable *non-financial indicator* which could be used to measure performance.

Activity or aspect to be measured

- Quality of installation service for kitchen units
- Output of carpets
- Customer satisfaction with a hotel
- Theatre ticket telephone booking service
- Website mail order books
- In-house accountancy training

7.5 Mann Ltd and Sett Ltd are two companies owned by Bow plc. Mann Ltd and Sett Ltd are similar companies using the same accounting policies. Both companies manufacture the same product, which is sold at the same price, to the house-building industry.

Financial and other information is given below for Mann Ltd, followed by certain performance indicators which have been calculated for Sett Ltd, for the year ended 31 March 2004.

Mann Ltd Income Statement: year to 31 March 2004

Units produced	15,000
Number of employees	12
	£000s
Turnover	1,750
Material and bought-in services	810
Production labour	210
Other production expenses	350
Depreciation – buildings	26
Depreciation – plant and machinery	90
Administration and other expenses	68
Operating profit	196

Mann Ltd: Extract from Balance Sheet as at 31 March 2004

	£000s	£000s	£000s
Fixed assets	Cost	Provision for Depreciation	NBV
Buildings	1,300	520	780
Plant and Machinery	900	540	360
	2,200	1,060	1,140
Net current assets			
Stock	34		
Debtors	27		
Cash	6		
Creditors	(42)		25
			1,165

Sett Ltd: Performance indicators for the year to 31 March 2004

- Units produced per employee (10 employees) 1,500
- Production labour cost per unit £12
- Added value per employee £95,000
- Asset turnover 0.8 times
- Operating profit margin 9.8%
- Return on capital employed 7.8%
- Operating profit per employee £17,150
- Units per £1,000 of NBV of Fixed Assets 7

Required:

(a) Calculate for Mann Ltd the eight performance indicators (as listed above for Sett Ltd) for the year ended 31 March 2004.

(b) Explain what is meant by 'productivity' and 'efficiency' when referring to a profit-making organisation.

(c) From the eight performance indicators used by Bow plc above, suggest two which best measure efficiency and state whether Mann Ltd or Sett Ltd is more efficient.

(d) From the eight performance indicators used by Bow plc above, suggest two which best measure productivity and state whether Mann Ltd or Sett Ltd has higher productivity.

(e) Explain briefly one reason why the indicators may show one company to be more efficient, but the other to have higher productivity.

7.6 CRS Ltd produces a single product, for which the standard direct labour time is 1.5 hours per unit. For a given period, CRS Ltd budgeted for a total of 33,600 hours. The actual results for the period showed that 22,000 units were produced and the actual total direct labour hours worked were 32,500 hours.

Required: State the formulae and calculate the Efficiency Ratio, the Capacity Ratio and the Activity Ratio for CRS Ltd for this period.

7.7 You are employed by Park Ltd, a company with several subsidiaries and you have been asked to apply the balanced scorecard to monitor the performance of the subsidiaries. The following information relates to Subsidiary Green for the year ended 31 October 2004.

Subsidiary Green Profit and Loss Account for the year to 31 October 2004

	£000s	£000s
Sales		5,200
Less: returns		200
Turnover		5,000
Less: Cost of Sales		
Opening Finished Stock	140	
Cost of Production	1,800	
Closing Finished Stock	(170)	1,770
Gross Profit		3,230
Administration	340	
Product Development	410	
Selling and Distribution	290	
Customer Services	360	
Training	200	1,600
Operating Profit		1,630

Results of inspection of finished goods show that 2% are found to be faulty and are scrapped.

Analysis of turnover by products:

Sales of new products	2,100
Sales of existing products	2,900
Turnover as above	5,000

Analysis of turnover by customers:

Sales to new customers	1,250
Sales to existing customers	3,750
Turnover as above	5,000

Required:

(a)   Identify and calculate, from the available information, one performance indicator which you could use in monitoring the financial perspective.

(b)   Explain briefly what is meant by:

- The *customer perspective*

- The *internal perspective*

- The *innovation and learning perspective*

For each of these three perspectives, identify and calculate two possible performance indicators from the information given for Subsidiary Green.

7.8   You are employed by Micro Circuits Ltd as a financial analyst. One of your responsibilities is to monitor the performance of subsidiaries within the group. Financial and other data relating to subsidiary A is reproduced below.

Subsidiary A
Profit and Loss Account for the year to 30 November 2008

	£000s	£000s
Sales		4,000
Less returns		100
Turnover (note 1)		3,900
Material	230	
Labour	400	
Production overheads (note 2)	300	
Cost of production	930	
Opening finished stock	50	
Closing finished stock	(140)	
Cost of Sales		840
Gross Profit		3,060
Marketing	500	
Customer support	400	
Research and Development	750	
Training	140	
Administration	295	2,085
Operating Profit		975

Extract from Balance Sheet at 30 November 2008

Fixed Assets	£000s Land and Buildings	£000s Plant and Machinery	£000s Total
Cost	2,000	2,500	4,500
Additions	–	1,800	1,800

	2,000	4,300	6,300
Accumulated depreciation	160	1,700	1,860
	1,840	2,600	4,440

Raw material stock	15
Finished goods stock	140
	155
Debtors	325
Cash and Bank	40
Creditors	(85)
	435
Net assets	4,875

Notes

1 Analysis of Turnover

	£000s		£000s
Regular customers	3,120	New products	1,560
New customers	780	Existing products	2,340
	3,900		3,900

2 Production overheads include £37,200 of reworked faulty production

3 Orders received in the year totalled £4,550,000

Required:

Calculate the following performance indicators for Subsidiary A for the year to 30 November 2008:

(a) the return on capital employed

(b) the asset turnover

(c) the sales (or operating profit) margin

(d) the average age of debtors in months

(e) the average age of finished stock in months

(f) **two** performance indicators, for which the data is already recorded, which could be used to measure quality in Micro Circuits Ltd subsidiaries. Show how your suggested indicators would be calculated

(g) the average delay in fulfilling orders

7.9   Allen Ltd is a wholesaler of electrical goods. The operating statement for Allen Ltd for the year ended 31 December 2004 is shown below, together with a simplified Balance Sheet as at that date.

The managers of Allen Ltd are concerned about the company's bank account being overdrawn and are considering improving the control of debtors and reducing the company's costs. They require the Operating Statement and the Balance Sheet to be re-drafted to show what the results would have been if all the following conditions had been applied:

- the debtors' payment period had been reduced to 1 month
- the administration costs had been reduced by £24,000
- the selling and distribution costs had been reduced by £6,000

Allen Ltd Operating Statement for the year ended 31 December 2004

	£000s	£000s
Turnover		468
Less: Cost of Sales		
Opening Stock	55	
Purchases	250	
Less: closing stock	(24)	281
Gross Profit		187
Administration Costs	92	
Selling and Distribution expenses	46	138
Operating profit		49

Allen Ltd Balance Sheet as at 31 December 2004

	£000s	£000s
Fixed Assets at cost		360
Less: accumulated depreciation		150
		210
Current Assets:		
Stock	24	
Debtors	69	
Cash at Bank	-	
	93	
Current Liabilities:		
Creditors	52	
Bank overdraft	11	
	63	
Net current assets		30
		240

Financed by:

Ordinary shares issued and fully paid	160
Retained Profits	80
	240

Required:

For Allen Ltd for the year ended 31 December 2004:

(a)   Calculate the following ratios from the given data:

- Gross Profit as a percentage of Turnover
- Operating Profit as a percentage of Turnover
- Return on Capital Employed
- Asset Turnover

(b)   Re-draft the Operating Statement and the Balance Sheet according to the three requirements of the managers of Allen Ltd.

(c)   Calculate the same four ratios as in (a) for the revised data prepared in (b).

(d)   Comment briefly on the results of your calculations.

7.10   Ravensdale is a nursing home run by a charitable trust. There are currently 30 residents. The following data relates to Ravensdale for the year ended 31 March 2004.

Ravensdale Operating Statement for the year ended 31 March 2004

	£	£
Income from Fees		546,000
Less: expenses		
Care of residents		
(variable with number of residents)	270,000	
Management and administration	55,000	
General expenses	81,000	
Depreciation of equipment and vehicles	88,000	494,000
Operating surplus		52,000

Ravensdale Summary of Net Assets as at 31 March 2004

	Premises	Equipment & vehicles	Total
Fixed Assets	£	£	£
Cost	980,000	440,000	1,420,000
Depreciation to date		176,000	176,000
	980,000	264,000	1,244,000
Current assets			
Debtors	68,250		
Cash at bank	30,450		
	98,700		
Creditors (for General Expenses)	13,500		
Net current assets			85,200
Net assets			1,329,200

Required:

(a)   Calculate:

   (i)   debtors' collection period in months

   (ii) payment period for creditors (which all relate to general expenses) in months

   (iii) total cash-based expenses (expenses other than depreciation)

   (iv) the number of months of cash based expenses that could be paid from the cash at bank

(b)   The following changes will take place in the next year (the year ended 31 March 2005):

   •   there will be 3 more residents and, as a result, fee income and the cost of care of residents will both increase by 10%

   •   new equipment will be purchased at a cost of £60,000 and the total depreciation charge (on equipment and vehicles) for the year will be £100,000

   •   the debtors' collection period will be reduced to 1 month

   •   the creditors' payment period will be reduced to 1.5 months

Taking account of all these changes, prepare a forecast operating statement and summary of net assets for Ravensdale for the year ended 31 March 2005.

Hint:

Net assets at 31 March 2005 =

Net assets at 31 March 2004 + surplus for the year ended 31 March 2005

After using this equation, cash at bank can be found as a balancing figure.

8 USING BUDGETS

8.1 List and explain briefly **three** of the main advantages of budgeting for an organisation.

8.2 Explain what is meant by the term 'key (or principal) budget factor'. What is the most common key budget factor for a manufacturing company? Suggest a possible key budget factor for a charity.

8.3 The deseasonalised data for sales volumes of product Alpha for the four quarters of Year 3 is as follows:

Quarter 1: 20,400 units
Quarter 2: 20,715 units
Quarter 3: 21,020 units
Quarter 4: 21,300 units

The average percentage seasonal variations in sales volume for Alpha have been calculated as:

Quarter	1	2	3	4
	−20%	−10%	−	+30%

Required:

Calculate the forecast sales volume of Alpha for each of the four quarters of Year 4, assuming that the year 3 trend and the average seasonal variations will continue.

8.4 The actual sales revenue for product Beta for the four quarters of Year 3 was as follows:

Quarter 1: £53,600
Quarter 2: £56,650
Quarter 3: £62,610
Quarter 4: £64,600

The average absolute (additive) seasonal variations in sales revenue for Beta have been calculated as:

Quarter	1	2	3	4
	− £5,000	− £2,500	+ £3,000	+ £4,500

Required:

(a) Calculate the deseasonalised trend in sales revenue for product Beta for Year 3.

(b) Calculate the forecast sales revenue for Beta for each of the four quarters of Year 4, assuming that the Year 3 trend and the average seasonal variations will continue.

(c) Explain briefly any reservations you may have about the validity of the forecasts in answer (b).

8.5   In Year 3, the direct materials used by a manufacturer of plumbing accessories included:

       Material W: at £3.20 per kg

       Material X: at £8.50 per kg

and the average wages paid included:

       Skilled production wages: £6.80 per hour

       Supervisors: £22,000 per annum.

The following index numbers are available:

	Year 3	Year 4 forecast
Plumbing accessory prices	103	102
Materials prices (type W)	128	130
Materials prices (type X)	115	119
National average wages	187	190

Required:

(a)   Calculate forecast costs for Year 4, for the materials and wages listed above.

(b)   Explain briefly any reservations you may have about the forecasts calculated in (a).

8.6   Boxco Ltd is a manufacturer of heavy-duty cardboard packing cases. Two sheets of cardboard are required to make each packing case. The following forecasts are available for January 2004:

Forecast sales demand = 1,750 packing cases

Stocks as at:	1 January 2004	31 January 2004
Finished packing cases	550	500
Cardboard sheets	880	920

Required:

(a)   For Boxco Ltd for January 2004, calculate the following:
  * production budget in units (packing cases)
  * materials usage budget in units (cardboard sheets)
  * materials purchases budget in units (cardboard sheets)

(b)   By considering the methods you have used in part (a), enter suitable formulae in the blank cells in columns B and C of the following spreadsheet format.

	A	B	C
1	Month	January	February
2	Sales forecast (packing cases)	1,750	2,000
3	Opening Finished Goods Stock	550	
4	Closing Finished Goods Stock	500	540
5	Production units (packing cases)		
6	Material usage per product unit	2	
7	Material usage for month (sheets)		
8	Opening Material Stock (sheets)	880	
9	Closing Material Stock (sheets)	920	950
10	Material Purchases units (sheets)		

8.7 Sunny Ltd is a manufacturer of moulded plastic toys. The standard cost of a garden toy is as follows:

0.9 kg of plastic at £0.80 per kg

0.25 hours of direct labour at £6.60 per hour

Fixed production overheads absorbed at £3.50 per unit

(Absorption rate based on budgeted production of 7,500 toys per quarter)

The selling price of this toy is £9.00.

The forecast sales volumes for this toy for the first three months of the year 2004 are:

	January	February	March
Sales units (toys)	1,800	2,000	2,300

The stock levels as at 1 January 2004 are planned to be:

Finished goods stock: 200 toys

Raw materials stock: 750 kg of plastic

It is planned to increase finished goods stocks by 200 toys per month and increase raw materials stocks by 100 kg per month, in anticipation of higher sales in Summer.

Required:

(a) Calculate the following for each of the first three months of 2004 and in total for the quarter:

- The production volume budget (number of toys)

- The raw materials usage budget in kg of plastic and in £

- The raw materials purchases budget in kg of plastic and in £

- The direct labour utilisation budget in hours and in £

(b) Using your answers to (a) set out a quarterly budgeted manufacturing and trading account for the quarter ended 31 March 2004 for this toy (ie using totals calculated in (a) for the quarter). Use absorption costing and show the adjustment to gross profit for any over or under absorption of fixed production overheads which would occur in this quarter.

8.8 Alder Ltd manufactures two products, AL1 and AL2, both of which are made from two materials, X and Y. The following data relates to Alder Ltd's next budget period.

Raw materials:	X	Y
Opening stock	8,000 kg	6,000 kg
Closing stock	11,000 kg	4,500 kg
Price per kg	£2.60	£4.10

Product:	AL1	AL2
Forecast sales (units)	12,500	15,000
Opening stock (units)	2,000	2,000
Closing stock (units)	4,000	1,000
Material X per product unit	2.0 kg	3.0 kg
Material Y per product unit	1.5 kg	2.0 kg
Direct labour hours per product unit	0.5 hours	1.5 hours

The total cost of Direct Labour is a step cost:

£165,000 for up to 27,500 hours

£175,000 for more than 27,500 and up to 29,000 hours

£185,000 for more than 29,000 and up to 30,500 hours

Required:

Calculate for Alder Ltd for the given budget period

(a)   the production volume required for each of the products AL1 and AL2

(b)   the quantities of each of the materials X and Y required for production

(c)   the quantities of each of the materials X and Y to be purchased

(d)   the total hours of direct labour required

(e)   the material purchases budget in £ for each of the materials X and Y

(f)   the total cost of direct labour for the period

8.9 Briar Ltd manufactures two products, BR1 and BR2, both of which are made from two materials, W and Z. Forecast total sales for the next year are 78,400 units of BR1 and 60,000 units of BR2. Analysis has shown that sales of BR1 are evenly spread through the year, but sales of BR2 are subject to additive (absolute) quarterly seasonal variations. The variations in sales of BR2 around the average are expected to be:

Quarter	1	2	3	4
Seasonal variation (units of BR2)	-800	+400	+700	-300

The following data for Briar Ltd relates to the budget for Quarter 1 of the next year.

Raw materials:	W	Z
Opening stock	10,000 kg	5,600 kg
Closing stock	9,000 kg	6,200 kg
Price per kg	£8.00	£1.80

Product:	BR1	BR2
Opening stock (units)	8,200	2,800
Closing stock (units)	4,000	3,000
Material W per product unit	4.0 kg	2.5 kg
Material Z per product unit	0.7 kg	1.2 kg
Direct labour hours per product unit	2.0 hours	1.5 hours

Direct Labour is a variable cost: £5.85 per hour. In addition to the hours required for production, 1,500 hours are to be allowed for training, to be paid at the same rate.

Required:

Calculate for Briar Ltd for Quarter 1 of the next year

(a)   the expected sales volume for each of the products BR1 and BR2

(b)   the production volume required for each of the products BR1 and BR2

(c)   the quantities of each of the materials W and Z required for production

(d)   the quantities of each of the materials W and Z to be purchased

(e)   the total hours of direct labour required for production

(f)   the material purchases budget in £ for each of the materials W and Z

(g)   the total cost of direct labour for the period

8.10   Cork Ltd manufactures two products, C and K, using the same material, M. The price of material M is forecast to rise significantly and the managers of Cork Ltd have decided to budget for no more than £252,000 to be spent on Material M in a four-week period. For the next four-week budget period, Cork Ltd will have opening stocks of 1,000 kg of M and will require closing stocks of 500 kg. There will be no opening or closing stocks of the finished products C and K.

Cork Ltd is contracted to sell 4,000 units of C in the period and will use any remaining material M to make as many units of product K as possible.

The materials and labour required for the two products are as follows:

Product	C	K
Direct material M per product unit	3 kg	5 kg
Direct labour hours per product unit	0.50 hours	1.25 hours

Cork Ltd has 32 direct workers, who normally work 39 hours per week. Overtime is used for any further hours required.

The price of material M was £9.00 per kg when a suitable index was at 108. The index is expected to be 126 in the next four-week budget period.

Required:

For Cork Ltd for the next four-week budget period, calculate

(a)   the expected price per kg of material M

(b)   the quantity of material M that can be purchased

(c)   the quantity of material M that can be used in production of product K

(d)   the number of units of product K that can be made and sold

(e)   the total direct labour hours required for products C and K during the period

(f)   the number of hours of overtime required

9 PRACTICAL ASPECTS OF BUDGET PREPARATION

9.1 The forecast demand for a component for a given period is 7,600 units. It is known that on average 5% of the finished components are rejected on final inspection.

If finished component stock levels are to remain unchanged, calculate the required units to be produced.

9.2 The forecast demand for a product for a given period is 5,300 units. The opening finished goods stock is 800 units and the required closing stock is 300 units. It is known that 4% of the product units on average are faulty and have to be scrapped.

Calculate the total production budget in units.

9.3 The standard direct labour time for a product is 2 hours per unit. 9,750 units of the product are to be produced in a given period. A new training initiative is to be brought in during the period, which will result in 2.5% of the direct labour time being used for training.

Calculate the total direct labour hours to be budgeted for the period.

9.4 The standard direct labour time for a product is 1 hour per product unit. Required production in a given period is 2,200 units. Following a new agreement on working methods, it is expected that 110% efficiency will be achieved in this period.

Calculate the labour hours to be budgeted for the required production.

9.5 The sales demand for a product in the next six months is expected to be 13,000 units. The opening finished goods stock is expected to be 1,460 units, and it is required to have 1,000 units in stock at the end of the six month period. On average, 5% of the units produced are rejected on inspection. The standard direct labour hours are 1.5 hours per unit, but this is a relatively new product and only 90% efficiency is expected in the period.

Calculate the hours to be budgeted for direct labour for the six month period.

9.6 Party Ltd is a manufacturer of paper plates. In cutting and forming the plates, 22% of the paper material is wasted. After cutting and forming, 2% of the plates have faults and are scrapped. Each batch of 100 finished plates weighs 1 kg and consists entirely of the paper material.

For the next period of production, the opening and closing stock levels are to be as follows:

	Paper (raw material)	Plates (finished goods)
Opening stock	200 kg	20,360 plates
Closing stock	350 kg	19,000 plates

The demand for finished plates for the period is 460,000 plates.

Required:

Calculate:

- the good production required
- the total production required
- the amount of paper needed to commence production
- the amount of paper required to be purchased

9.7   Green Ltd is a manufacturer of garden furniture. The forecast monthly demand for its garden chairs for the year 2004 is as follows:

2004 Forecast sales volume (Number of chairs):

January	3,000	July	25,000
February	8,000	August	20,000
March	15,000	September	15,000
April	20,000	October	4,000
May	20,000	November	2,000
June	25,000	December	2,000

Green Ltd's stock policy is to have 30% of the next month's demand in stock at the end of each month. The stock of chairs at 1 January 2004 and at 31 December 2004 is expected to be 900 chairs. The direct labour hours available per month in Green Ltd (without any overtime working) are sufficient to make 22,000 chairs.

Required:

(a)   Calculate the required monthly production of chairs in line with Green Ltd's stock policy.

(b)   (i)   Explain how production could be rescheduled in order to avoid the necessity for overtime. State the monthly production required to do this without stock levels falling below the levels stated in the current policy.

(ii)   State the closing stock of chairs at the end of each month in your revised production schedule.

(c)   What further information would you require in order to decide whether it would be better for Green Ltd to reschedule production or to use direct labour overtime to complete the production according to the original budget?

(d)   Suggest two other alternative courses of action open to the management of Green Ltd, which would enable them to satisfy the demand for their garden chairs.

9.8 Kale Ltd manufactures two products, K and L, using two materials, U and V. The following data relates to Kale Ltd for the next budget period.

Product	K	L
Sales (units)	5,950	7,600
Opening stock (units)	200	750
Closing stock (units)	250	750
Material U per product unit of output	-	0.5 m
Material V per product unit of output	2.0 m	1.0 m
Direct labour per product unit	1.0 hours	0.8 hours

Material	U	V
Opening stock	900 m	800 m
Closing stock	500 m	1,400 m
Wastage during production	5%	2%

Required:

Calculate for Kale Ltd for the next budget period

(a) production volume required for each of the products K and L

(b) quantity of each of the materials U and V required for production output

(c) quantity of each of the materials U and V for input to production

(d) quantity of each of the materials U and V to be purchased

(e) the direct labour hours required for production

(f) the total direct labour hours to be paid for, if an additional 2% of production time is to be allowed for setting up machinery

9.9 Lewis Ltd manufactures two products, Jay and Kay, using the same material and the same direct labour force. The original budget data for the next quarter is as follows. There is no budgeted finished goods stock at the beginning or end of the quarter. Fixed overheads are absorbed on the basis of £30 per product unit.

Product	Demand	Costs per unit		
		Direct material	Direct labour	Fixed overhead
Jay	2,840 units	£56	£18	£30
Kay	3,360 units	£50	£14	£30

The material costs £4 per kg. Direct material and direct labour are variable costs. The selling prices of the products are £127 per unit of Jay and £120 per unit of Kay.

The direct material used by Lewis Ltd is in short supply and the company will be able to obtain only 70,000 kg for production in the next quarter. The direct labour hours needed for full production are available.

Required:

(a)   Calculate the quantity of material that would be needed by Lewis Ltd for production of the full demand for Jay and Kay in the next quarter.

(b)   Taking into account the limit on the supply of material, produce a revised production budget in units for the next quarter that maximises profit for Lewis Ltd.

(c)   Calculate the total budgeted contribution that Lewis Ltd would obtain in the next quarter using your production budget from (b) and assuming all production is sold.

(d)   Calculate the total budgeted fixed overhead and the budgeted profit for Lewis Ltd for the next quarter, using your answer to part (c).

9.10 Glynn Ltd manufactures three products, L, Y and N, using the same material and the same two grades of direct labour.

The original budget data for the next quarter is as follows. There is no budgeted finished goods stock at the beginning or end of the quarter.

Product	Demand	Variable Costs per unit		
		Direct material	Direct labour Grade I	Direct labour Grade II
L	7,800 units	£32	£32	£27
Y	3,800 units	£44	£48	£54
N	8,000 units	£23	£16	£6

Supplies of the material are unlimited. Direct material and both grades of direct labour are variable costs. The selling prices of the products are £210 per unit of L, £300 per unit of Y and £100 per unit of N.

The Grade II direct labour hours needed for full production are available, but Grade I workers are currently in short supply. Glynn Ltd has started a training programme to improve the situation. There are two cases to consider for the next quarter, depending on the number of trainees completing the training programme:

(i) 58,000 Grade I direct labours hours will be available

(ii) 70,250 Grade I direct labour hours will be available

The direct labour rate for Grade I is £6.40 per hour. The fixed costs amount to £1,250,000 per quarter.

Required:

(a)   Calculate the contribution per unit for each of the products L, Y and N

(b)   Calculate the contribution per unit per hour of Grade I direct labour for each of the products and hence rank the products for best use of this limited resource

(c)   For each of the cases (i) and (ii), prepare revised production budgets in units to maximise profit for the next quarter

(d)   Calculate the total contribution and hence the profit resulting from each of your answers in part (c)

(e)   Comment briefly on the factors other than quarterly profit maximisation that the managers of Glynn Ltd should take into account when setting production budgets during the period of shortage of Grade I labour

10 APPLICATION OF BUDGETING METHODS

10.1 Incremental budgeting is used by Pastel Papers Ltd, a company which manufactures stationery products. Company administration salaries for last year amounted to £180,000. The company has expansion plans which are expected to result in £30,000 of additional administration salaries (estimated at current prices). Forecast inflation is expected to result in a 2% increase in such salaries.

What would be the Pastel Papers Ltd budget for administration salaries for the coming year, using incremental budgeting?

10.2 (a) List and explain briefly the advantages and disadvantages of incremental budgeting.

(b) In what circumstances are

(i) zero base budgeting

(ii) programme based budgeting

most likely to be appropriate?

10.3 Production overheads in a manufacturing company have been identified as semi-variable. They consist of fixed costs of £220,000 plus £5.10 per unit produced, for a range of levels of production from 25,000 units to 40,000 units for the period.

Required:

(a) Calculate the total production overheads for

(i) 30,000 units of production

(ii) 36,500 units of production

(b) Why would the same method not be appropriate for calculating the production overheads for 20,000 units or 50,000 units?

10.4 You are given the total of a semi-variable cost at four different levels of activity, as follows:

Level of activity (units)	500	780	1,000	1,200
Total cost (£)	1,875	2,141	2,350	2,540

Use the high-low method to calculate the variable cost per unit and the fixed part of this semi-variable cost.

10.5   Yare Ltd manufactures a single product, the Yare, and the budgeted costs of production are as follows (for levels of production between 10,000 and 16,000 units of Yare):

Direct material is a variable cost: £5.20 per unit of Yare produced

Direct labour is a semi-variable cost: £35,000 fixed cost plus £8.50 per unit of Yare produced

Production overhead is a semi-variable cost: £40,000 fixed cost plus £4.80 per unit of Yare produced.

Required:

For Yare Ltd

(a)   Calculate the total costs of production for 12,000 units of Yare

(b)   Enter formulas in cells B8 to B12 of the following spreadsheet, so that it could be used to calculate the budgeted production costs for any number of units of Yare within the relevant range and with any budgeted fixed and variable costs. The given data is shown as an example.

		A	B
1	Production volume (units of Yare)		12,000
2	Direct material: variable cost per unit of Yare (£)		5.20
3	Direct labour: variable cost per unit of Yare (£)		8.50
4	Direct labour: fixed cost (£)		35,000
5	Production overhead: variable cost per unit of Yare (£)		4.80
6	Production overhead: fixed cost (£)		40,000
7	**Budgeted production cost:**		£
8	Direct material		
9	Direct labour		
10	Production overhead		
11	Total budgeted production cost		
12	Budgeted production cost per unit		

10.6   The Bure Company makes a single product, PB. Budgets have been prepared for the company's production costs at two levels of activity: 20,000 units or 35,000 units of PB, as shown below. In this range of levels of activity, the direct costs are either variable or semi-variable and the production overheads are semi-variable.

The Bure Company Budgeted Production Costs

Production (units of PB)	20,000	35,000
	£	£
Direct material	30,000	52,500
Direct labour	198,000	294,000
Production overheads	130,000	186,250
Total production cost	358,000	532,750

Required:

For The Bure Company, calculate:

(a) the fixed and variable parts of each type of cost, using the high-low method

(b) the flexible production cost budget for 30,000 units of PB

10.7 SP-CARS plc is a manufacturer of sports cars, and one of its divisions (Seats Division) makes seats for the cars. The seats are all transferred at cost to another division of SP-CARS plc, to be fitted into the cars. The demand for seats therefore depends on the total production of cars in SP-CARS plc.

For the year to 30 September 2004, Seats Division prepared two provisional budgets, as shown below. They have been prepared on a basis which would apply to any level of demand from 5,000 to 7,500 seats. Over this range, the first three elements of cost shown are either variable or semi-variable. 'Rent, insurance and depreciation' behaves as a step cost. It is fixed for production from 5,000 to 6,250 seats, but increases by £5,000 per year when production exceeds 6,250 seats.

Seats Division provisional budgets: 12 months to 30 September 2004

Volume (number of Seats)	6,000	7,000
	£	£
Material	108,000	126,000
Labour	150,000	165,000
Power and Maintenance	31,600	33,200
Rent, Insurance and Depreciation	85,000	90,000
Total cost	374,600	414,200

After these budgets were prepared, it was estimated that 6,000 seats would be required, and the first budget above was set as the budget for the year.

During the year ended 30 September 2004, SP-CARS plc actually needed 6,300 seats and a performance statement was prepared, as shown below.

Seats Division performance statement: 12 months to 30 September 2004

	Budget	Actual	Variance
Volume (number of Seats)	6,000	6,300	
	£	£	£
Material	108,000	110,000	2,000 A
Labour	150,000	160,500	10,500 A
Power and Maintenance	31,600	28,000	3,600 F
Rent, Insurance and Depreciation	85,000	88,000	3,000 A
Total cost	374,600	386,500	11,900 A

Note: F=Favourable, A=Adverse

Required:

(a) Using the data given in the two provisional budgets, calculate the fixed and variable cost elements for Material, Labour and Power and Maintenance.

(b) On investigation of the significant adverse labour variance, it is found that an error had occurred in coding the actual costs. Maintenance costs of £2,500 had been coded to Labour. Adjust the actual results to correct this error.

Using your answers to (a), prepare an amended performance statement based on flexible budgeting. Show a flexed budget compared with the corrected actual results to give the (revised) variances.

(c) Explain briefly, with reference to the case of SP-CARS plc, why a flexible budget is preferable to a fixed budget for measuring performance.

10.8 Hillfield Ltd commenced the manufacture and sale of a single product, coded HFD, on 1 July 2004.

The original budget for Hillfield Ltd for the 3 months to 30 September 2004 planned for production and sales volumes to be equal, both being 1,500 HFDs.

The actual results for the period were that 1,400 HFDs were produced and only 1,100 sold. The budgeted and actual figures are given below, together with attached notes.

Hillfield Ltd: Operating results for 3 months ending 30 September 2004

	Budget	Actual
Sales volume (HFDs)	1,500	1,100
Production volume (HFDs)	1,500	1,400
	£	£
Sales	60,000	46,200
Less: Cost of Sales:		
Direct costs:		
Materials	7,500	6,380
Labour	9,000	7,150
Overheads:		
Production overheads	13,450	10,442
Total production cost of sales	29,950	23,972
Selling overheads	16,350	15,660
Total cost of sales	46,300	39,632
Profit	13,700	6,568

Notes:

(i) Direct materials and direct labour are both variable costs.

(ii) Production overheads are semi-variable. The budget for the fixed part is £10,000 for this level of activity. The actual fixed production overhead incurred was equal to the budget.

(iii) Selling overheads are semi-variable. The budget for the fixed part is £15,000. The remainder varies in relation to sales volume. The actual fixed selling overhead was equal to the budget.

(iv) There were no stocks of work-in-progress and no opening stocks of finished goods.

(v)   To calculate the actual cost of sales in the statement above, the closing stocks were valued at actual production cost. The number of HFDs was used to apportion the actual production costs between the cost of sales and the closing stock. The composition of the production cost of sales and closing stock was therefore:

	Closing Stock	Cost of Sales	Cost of Production
Number of units (HFDs)	300	1,100	1,400
	£	£	£
Direct material	1,740	6,380	8,120
Direct labour	1,950	7,150	9,100
Production overhead	2,848	10,442	13,290
Production cost	6,538	23,972	30,510

Required:

(a)   Calculate the following:

- the budgeted selling price per HFD

- the budgeted direct material cost per HFD

- the budgeted direct labour cost per HFD

- the budgeted marginal cost of production overhead per HFD

- the actual marginal cost of production overhead per HFD

- the budgeted marginal cost of selling overhead per HFD

- the actual marginal cost of selling overhead per HFD

(b)   Prepare a flexible budget statement for the operating results of Hillfield Ltd for the 3 months to 30 September 2004, using marginal costing format and showing the variances.

(c)   Explain briefly why the actual profit reported in the marginal costing statement for the 3 months to 30 September 2004 for Hillfield Ltd differs from the actual profit shown in the original statement. Show how the two profit figures can be reconciled.

10.9   State whether each of the following is TRUE or FALSE.

1   Zero base budgeting encourages changes in working methods.

2   Zero base budgeting encourages the introduction of budgetary slack into budgets.

3   A cost which is a constant amount per unit is described as fixed.

4   Marginal costing uses a cost for each unit of output based purely on variable costs.

5   A control period is the length of time for which a budget is prepared, usually a year.

6   It is not worthwhile to investigate favourable variances.

7   Comparing actual results with a flexible budget gives useful feedback for control purposes.

8   Feedforward might result in a revised version of the budget.

9   Variances which exceed the control limits should be identified and reported to the manager responsible.

10   Management reports should not include any non-financial information.

10.10 Bond plc is a manufacturer of robotic machines. The managers of Bond plc are considering developing a new machine. The machine would have a relatively short life cycle, for which the following forecasts have been made:

- research, development and design would cost £6.5million

- sales would take place over the following 3 years

- production costs would be £2.2million per year for 3 years plus £19,000 per unit

- customer support would cost £1million per year for 3 years

- the total sales demand for the machine over the whole of its life cycle has been estimated as 900 units at £55,000 each

Required:

(a) Calculate for the new machine being considered by Bond plc

(i) the total budgeted life cycle sales revenue from the machine

(ii) the total budgeted life cycle costs of the machine (assuming production and sales volumes are equal)

(iii) the total budgeted life cycle profit from the machine

(b) Explain briefly the advantages of life cycle budgeting for this type of product.

11 MANAGEMENT ISSUES IN RELATION TO BUDGETING

11.1 Management Accounting information is useful to managers for:

- reporting results

- highlighting problems that need action

- assisting with decision-making

Required:

(a) For each of the three purposes given above, give two examples of management accounting information which could be used.

(b) Explain briefly why management information is important to the senior managers of a large organisation.

(c) What is the starting point for the planning process for an organisation?

11.2 The following are short extracts from a Police Authority Budget and Performance Plan for the year 2004/2005.

1 the Authority's five-year Best Value programme is flexible and dynamic and is reviewed each year

2 investing in information technology and essential support services including dedicated police air support coverage

3 securing the maintenance of an efficient and effective police service throughout the county

4 making more police officers available for frontline duties

5 answer 90% of '999' calls within 10 seconds

6 minimum police strength of 1,475 officers by 31 March 2005

7 the Constabulary delivers service to clear standards covering both cost and quality

8 attend 88% of incidents requiring immediate response in rural areas within 20 minutes

9 responding to the community's request for more visible and accessible policing, thus reducing the fear of crime

10 no more violent crimes in this year in public places than in 2003/2004

Required: with reference to the extracts given above:

(a) Explain the term 'best value'.

(b) For each of the given extracts, state whether it relates to:
- long-term organisational goals or objectives
- strategies for achieving objectives
- short-term aims

(c) Explain briefly, using your answer to (b) as an illustration, how the long-term goals of an organisation can be expressed in short-term detailed budgets for sections of the organisation.

(d) Identify four measures of performance which could be used in the annual review, in which the level of achievement of the stated aims is assessed.

11.3 Required:

(a) Explain what is meant by the term 'controllable cost'.

(b) Explain why it is important for performance measurement to identify whether a cost is controllable by a particular manager.

11.4 The following information relates to Astro Screens Ltd, a manufacturer of computer screens. The company's organisational goals include continuous quality improvements as well as maximisation of profits.

There are four screen production departments, (SP1 – SP4), each making a particular type of screen. Department G produces a component which is transferred to the four SP departments, where it is used in the manufacture of the screens. The components are transferred at standard production cost and are not sold to other customers. The manager of Department G is responsible for the direct cost variances relating to production of the component.

Astro Screens Ltd has contracts to supply screens to ten computer manufacturers. Due to frequent changes in product specifications, the contracts are short-term and prices are re-negotiated by the managers of the SP (screen production) departments on a regular basis. The managers of the SP departments have responsibility for ensuring that the quality and delivery dates of supplies to customers can be guaranteed. They have the authority to appoint the skilled staff needed and arrange staff overtime. They are also authorised to invest in machinery or equipment necessary to do this, up to an agreed maximum for each department.

Required:

(a) For department G of Astro Screens Ltd, state whether it can be considered as

- a cost centre
- a profit centre
- an investment centre

(b) For department G of Astro Screens Ltd, suggest one reason why the transfer of components at standard production cost may not result in goal congruence.

(c) For the SP (screen production) departments of Astro Screens Ltd, state whether each department can be considered as

- a cost centre
- a profit centre
- an investment centre

(d) For the SP departments of Astro Screens Ltd, state whether the following items can be considered as controllable by each departmental manager

- sales revenue
- cost of components transferred from department G
- direct labour cost

(e)   For the SP departmental managers in Astro Screens Ltd, suggest one financial and one non-financial measure of performance.

11.5 For the year ended 31 March 2004, the senior manager of North County Library Services introduced participative budgeting for the managers of main and branch libraries. Premises costs such as rent and rates and buildings maintenance are paid from a central budget for all the libraries in the county.

The following information relates to Eastwick (North County) Branch Library for the year ended 31 March 2004.

	Budget	Actual	Variance
	£	£	£
Library budget allocation	100,000	100,000	–
Other income (fines, charges photocopying, sales of maps, prints, old books etc.)	6,000	5,400	600 A
	106,000	105,400	600 A
Less:			
Staff salaries	85,000	85,600	600 A
Replacement books etc	7,800	7,650	150 F
Magazine subscriptions	3,200	3,350	150 A
Cleaning	2,600	2,700	100 A
Maintenance of fixtures	900	400	500 F
Depreciation of fixtures	1,800	1,800	–
Lease of photocopier	1,900	1,900	–
Heating and Lighting	2,800	2,000	800F
	106,000	105,400	600 F
Net surplus/deficit	nil	nil	nil

Required:

(a)   Explain briefly what 'participative budgeting' implies for library managers.

(b)   Suggest two reasons why the favourable variances shown above may have occurred, other than as a result of better motivation due to participative budgeting.

(c)   Under what circumstances is it likely to be preferable for a senior manager to impose a budget, rather than take the participative approach?

11.6   Topp plc uses divisional profits as the basis for performance related pay for its divisional managers. The company's objectives include becoming a market leader for a complete range of high quality products as well as satisfying its share-holders with good returns on their investment.

Required:

(a)   List three essential features for the success of Topp plc's performance related pay scheme.

(b)   Suggest how a performance related pay scheme based on profits might encourage Topp plc's divisional managers to take action which does not lead to goal congruence.

11.7   You have recently been appointed as accountant to Claude Ltd, a small company manufacturing a specialised fertiliser. Part of the process involves using ovens which must be kept at a constant temperature all the time, even when empty. The power to heat the ovens does not therefore vary with changes in the amount of fertiliser being produced and so the cost of power is treated as a fixed cost.

The managing director, Emile Claude, shows you the following cost reports for the year ended 30 November 2004 and for the last quarter of that year, commenting that:

- the reports are not helpful for the purpose of managing the business

- he cannot understand why the direct material variance for the fourth quarter is favourable, when he is aware that the cost per unit of the material has been increasing throughout the year

- the direct labour variances, being adverse for the year and favourable for the quarter, seem incorrect, because the production workers have been paid the budgeted rate of £8 per hour throughout the year and no overtime was worked

- he is concerned that the power costs are so high in the fourth quarter even though output was below the budget

Claude Ltd Cost Report for the year ended 30 November 2004

	Budget		Actual		Variance
Units produced (tonnes)	12,000		13,000		1,000 F
	£	£	£	£	£
Direct material		144,000		188,500	44,500 A
Direct labour		192,000		227,500	35,500 A
Fixed overheads:					
Lease of machinery	60,000		60,000		–
Rent and rates	96,000		104,000		8,000 A
Insurance	48,000		52,000		4,000 A
Power	120,000		140,000		20,000 A
		324,000		356,000	
Total costs		660,000		772,000	112,000 A

Claude Ltd Cost Report for Quarter 4 of the year ended 30 November 2004

		Budget		Actual	Variance
Units produced (tonnes)		3,000		2,400	600 A
	£	£	£	£	£
Direct material		36,000		35,280	720 F
Direct labour		48,000		42,240	5,760 F
Fixed overheads:					
Lease of machinery	15,000		15,000		–
Rent and rates	24,000		26,000		2,000 A
Insurance	12,000		13,000		1,000 A
Power	30,000		36,000		6,000 A
		81,000		90,000	
Total costs		165,000		167,520	2,520 A

Before answering the managing director's queries, you investigate the power cost and find out that, although not variable with output, the quarterly cost does vary because it is affected by the outside temperature. You find that the seasonal variations for the cost of power are on average:

Quarter 1	Quarter 2	Quarter 3	Quarter 4
+5%	-10%	-20%	+25%

Required:

Write a report to the managing director, answering his queries. Include cost reports for the year and for the quarter in a form that gives more useful information, explaining briefly the changes you have made.

11.8 It is 1 March and Professor Pauline Heath has just taken up her new appointment as the Head of the Postgraduate Business Studies Department in a new university. Due to unfilled vacancies throughout the current academic year, the department has had to rely on part-time academic staff. The cost of part-time staff who are self-employed is coded to account number 321, while those who are taxed under the Pay-As-You-Earn system are charged to account code 002. Both types of staff enter their claims within ten days of each month-end and these then appear in the management reports of the subsequent month. There are also unfilled clerical and administrative staff vacancies.

The university has a residential conference centre, which the department makes use of from time to time. Sometimes this is because the department's allocated rooms are all in use and sometimes because the department teaches at weekends. The charge for the use of the centre is coded to account 673. An alternative to using the conference centre is to hire outside facilities at local hotels, in which case the expenditure is coded to account 341.

The main forms of income are tuition fees and a higher education grant from the government. The extent of this grant is known before the commencement of the academic year and is payable in two parts, one-third at the end of December and the balance at the end of April.

One of Professor Heath's first tasks was to check the enrolments for the current year. The financial and academic year commenced on 1 September and is subdivided into three terms, each lasting four months. The Autumn term commenced on 1 September and the Spring term on 1 January. All courses commence at the beginning of the Autumn term, the MBA and MSc courses lasting three terms and the diploma course two terms.

The departmental administrator has presented Professor Heath with the enrolment data for the current academic year. Whilst absorbing this information, she has also received the latest management accounts for the department. Both sets of information are reproduced below and on the next page.

Professor Heath is experiencing difficulties in understanding the latest management report. She has written a memo to the university's finance director expressing her anxieties about the presentation of the report and its detailed contents.

Enrolment data-current academic year	Fee (£)	Enrolments	Income (£)
MBA – three terms	3,500	160	560,000
MSc – three terms	3,200	80	256,000
Diploma Course – two terms	1,200	100	120,000
			936,000

Required:

(a) (i) Rearrange the account headings into a more meaningful form for managers. This should include columnar headings for any financial data you feel is appropriate but you do not need to include any figures.

(ii) Briefly justify your proposals.

(b) In her memo, Professor Heath states that the current form of report does not help her manage her department. Identify the strengths and weaknesses apparent in the current system, other than the presentational ones covered in (a), and make and justify outline proposals that will help her manage the department.

(c) Referring to the detailed financial data under the heading of Income, reproduce the actual income to date in a form consistent with accounting principles.

workbook activities **73**

Department of Postgraduate Business Studies
Monthly Management Report – February

Code	Account heading	Annual budget	6 months to 28 February			Budget remaining
			Actual	Budget	Variance	
	Expenses					
001	Full-time academic	600,000	230,000	300,000	70,000	370,000
002	Part-time academic	84,000	48,000	42,000	-6,000	36,000
003	Clerical and administration	84,000	36,000	42,000	6,000	48,000
218	Teaching and learning material	30,000	0	15,000	15,000	30,000
321	Teaching and research fees	20,000	19,000	10,000	-9,000	1,000
331	Agency staff (clerical and administrative)	300	2,400	150	-2,250	-2,100
341	External room hire	1,000	400	500	100	600
434	Course advertising (press)	26,000	600	13,000	12,400	25,400
455	Postage and telephone recharge	8,000	1,200	4,000	2,800	6,800
673	Internal room hire	24,000	14,000	12,000	-2,000	10,000
679	Central services recharge	340,000	170,000	170,000	0	170,000
680	Rental light and heat recharge	260,000	130,000	130,000	0	130,000
		1,477,300	651,600	738,650	87,050	825,700
	Income					
802	Tuition fees	900,000	936,000	900,000	-36,000	-36,000
890	Higher education grant	750,000	250,000	250,000	0	500,000
		1,650,000	1,186,000	1,150,000	-36,000	464,000
	Net surplus/deficit	172,700	534,400	411,350	-123,050	-361,700

Practice Examinations

This section contains assessment tasks derived from past and specimen Examinations reproduced by kind permission of AAT.

Details of these practice examinations are set out on the next page.

PRACTICE EXAMINATIONS

Unit 33
Management Accounting

Practice examination 1
Merano Ltd, Blossom Ltd and Aspex Technologies Ltd

This examination paper is in THREE sections.

You must show competency in ALL sections.

You should therefore attempt and aim to complete EVERY task in EACH section.

You should spend about 60 minutes on Section 1 and 60 minutes on Section 2 and 60 minutes on Section 3.

Include all essential workings within your answers, where appropriate.

SECTION 1

You should spend about 60 minutes on this section.

DATA

You are employed as a management accountant by Merano Ltd and report to Louise Owen, the Finance Director. The company uses marginal (or variable) costing when preparing management accounts and divides the year into 20 day periods for both production and sales. One subsidiary, Solden Ltd, makes two products, the Exe and the Wye.

Louise Owen asks you to prepare Solden's budgets for period 1, the 20 days ending 26 January 2007.

Louise Owen gives you the following information.

Sales data	Units of Exe	Units of Wye
• Budgeted sales for period 1, 20 days ending 26 January	3,200	2,344
• Budgeted sales for period 2, 20 days ending 23 February	3,000	2,500

Stock data

• The opening finished stocks for period 1 will be 140 Exes and 184 Wyes.

• Closing finished stocks of Exe for period 1 must equal 2 days' sales in period 2.

• Closing finished stocks of Wye for period 1 must equal 4 days' sales in period 2.

• There is no stock of work-in-progress at any time.

Faulty production

• 4% of Exe finished production and 5% of Wye finished production is faulty and has to be destroyed. This faulty production has no value.

Task 1.1

Prepare a production budget for period 1, the 20 days ending 26 January 2007, showing the number of Exes and the number of Wyes to be produced, including any faulty production, to meet the budgeted sales in period 1.

DATA

After you prepared the production budget, Louise Owen tells you that:

• Exe and Wye use the same material.

• Each Exe requires 6 kilograms of material.

• Each Wye requires 8 kilograms of material.

• The material costs £20 per kilogram.

• The stock of material at the beginning of period 1 will be 2,000 kilograms.

• The stock of material at the end of period 1 will be 2,400 kilograms.

Task 1.2

Prepare the following budgets for period 1:

(a)   material purchases budget in kilograms

(b)   cost of materials budget

DATA

Louise Owen gives you the following additional information:

*   Exe and Wye use the same type of labour.

*   Each Exe requires 8 labour hours.

*   Each Wye requires 5 labour hours.

*   In any 20 day period, the workforce can work up to 40,000 labour hours before overtime.

*   The normal labour rate is £6 per hour.

*   The maximum overtime the employees in Solden can work is 4,000 labour hours.

*   If any overtime is worked, the labour rate is £9 per hour.

Task 1.3

Prepare the following budgets for period 1:

(a)   labour hours budget, including any idle time or overtime to be worked

(b)   cost of labour budget, including any overtime to be paid

DATA

Louise Owen has to discuss the budgeted results of Solden with her other directors and asks for your help in preparing the information. She gives you the following information.

*   Solden uses marginal (or variable) costing when preparing reports for directors.

*   Any idle time or overtime is charged to fixed overheads.

*   The budgeted selling price of each Exe is £200.

*   The budgeted selling price of each Wye is £250.

*   The opening stocks of 140 Exes, 184 Wyes and 2,000 kilograms of materials have the same unit costs as in period 1.

Task 1.4

Prepare the following statements for period 1:

(a)   the budgeted marginal (or variable) cost of production for each product

(b)   the unit cost of fault-free production for each product

(c)   a budgeted operating statement showing for each product the total turnover, total expenses and total contribution.

DATA

After preparing the budgets, Louise Owen tells you that:

* Solden now believes it can sell an extra 220 Exes in period 1.

* Total overtime cannot be more than the hours given in Task 1.3 and labour hours cannot be increased in any other way.

* The maximum extra material available for period 1 is 1,200 kilograms.

Task 1.5

Calculate:

(a) the maximum extra production of fault-free units of Exe possible if labour hours were the only constraint

(b) the maximum extra production of fault-free units of Exe possible if material were the only constraint

(c) the revised fault-free production of Exes in period 1

SECTION 2

You should spend about 60 minutes on this section.

DATA

Blossom Ltd manufactures and sells garden statues. You work as an accounting technician reporting to the Finance Director. The company uses a standard cost stock system.

The actual and budgeted results for the production department for November are as follows:

Production Department: Actual and Budgeted Results for November 2006

		Actual		*Budget*
Production		6,500 units		7,500 units
		£		£
Materials	20,800 kgs	91,520	22,500 kgs	90,000
Labour	7,150 hours	44,330	7,500 hours	45,000
Fixed overheads		15,850		15,000
Total production cost		151,700		150,000

Fixed production overheads are absorbed using a budgeted overhead absorption rate per labour hour.

Task 2.1

(a)   Calculate the following information for November:

  (i)   standard price of materials per kg

  (ii)   actual price of materials per kg

  (iii)   standard usage of materials for actual production

  (iv)   standard labour rate per hour

  (v)   actual labour rate per hour

  (vi)   standard labour hours for actual production

  (vii) budgeted overhead absorption rate

(b)   Calculate the following variances for November:

  (i)   the material price variance

  (ii)   the material usage variance

  (iii)   the labour rate variance

  (iv)   the labour efficiency variance

  (v)   the fixed overhead expenditure variance

  (vi)   the fixed overhead volume variance

  (vii) the fixed overhead capacity variance

  (viii) the fixed overhead efficiency variance

(c)   Using the variances you have calculated in Task 2.1(b), prepare an operating statement for November which reconciles the standard absorption cost of total actual production with the actual absorption cost of total actual production.

SECTION 3

You should spend about 60 minutes on this section.

DATA

You are employed as an accounting technician by Aspex Technologies Ltd. One of your duties is to prepare performance indicators and other information for Stuart Morgan, the Financial Director.

Aspex Technologies make a single product, the Zeta. In the year to 30 November 2006 the company has had problems with the quality of the material used to make Zetas and Stuart would like to know what the *cost of quality* has been for the year.

The *cost of quality* is defined as the total of all costs incurred in preventing faults plus those costs involved in correcting faults once they have occurred. It is a single figure measuring all the explicit costs of quality – that is, those costs collected within the accounting system.

Stuart provides you with the following financial statements and data.

Operating statement – year ended 30 November 2006

	Units	£000	£000
Turnover	360,000		14,400
Purchases	400,000	6,400	
Less returns	(40,000)	(640)	
Net purchases	360,000	5,760	
Add opening stocks	90,000	1,440	
Less closing stocks	(90,000)	(1,440)	
Material issued to production	360,000	5,760	
Production labour		3,600	
Variable cost of production and sales			9,360
Contribution			5,040
Heat, light and power		720	
Depreciation		1,000	
Inspection cost		80	
Production overhead		2,000	
Reworking of faulty production		40	
Customer Support		200	
Marketing and administrative expenses		424	
Total fixed overheads			4,464
Operating profit			576

Balance sheet at 30 November 2006

	£000	£000
Fixed assets at cost		8,000
Cumulative depreciation		2,000
Net book value		6,000
Stock of materials	1,440	
Debtors	2,400	
Cash	960	
Creditors	(1,200)	
Net current assets		3,600
		9,600
Financed by		
Debt		6,000
Equity		3,600
		9,600

- The number of production employees in the company is 180.
- Production labour is a variable expense.
- The demand for Zetas in the year to 30 November 2006 was 390,000 but not all could be produced and sold due to poor quality materials. Any orders not completed this year can be completed next year.
- The only reason for the reworking of faulty production and customer support expenses was the poor quality of the materials.
- Material and heat, light and power are the only bought-in expenses.
- Creditors relate entirely to material purchases.
- There are no stocks of finished goods or work in progress.
- Depreciation is based on the straight line method.

Task 3.1

Prepare the following information for Stuart Morgan:

(a)   selling price per Zeta

(b)   material cost per Zeta

(c)   labour cost per Zeta

(d)   contribution per Zeta

(e)   contribution percentage

(f)   net profit (or sales) margin

(g)   return on capital employed

(h)   asset turnover

(i)   average age of debtors in months

(j)   average age of stock in months

(k)   average age of creditors in months

(l)   added value per employee

(m)   average delay in completing an order in months

(n)   cost of quality

DATA

Stuart Morgan tells you that the Directors of Aspex Technologies have agreed an action plan for the year to 30 November 2007. The plan involves:

- using market research to forecast likely sales volume and prices
- implementing total quality management and just-in-time stock control
- greater working capital control

Stuart provides you with the following information:

Market research

- Indices for this year and next year

	Selling Price Index	Sales Volume Index
Indices for year ended 30 November 2006	180	70
Forecast indices for year ending 30 November 2007	171	84

- The *total* forecast sales volume for the year ending 30 November 2007 is made up of two elements:

    – a revised volume from applying the sales volume indices to the 360,000 Zetas sold in the year to 30 November 2006

    – an additional volume from completing orders placed in the year to 30 November 2006 but not made in that year because of the poor quality materials

- The forecast selling price applies to the *total* forecast sales volume using the selling price indices.

Total quality management and just-in-time stock control

- The material supplier has agreed to take back the existing closing stock and replace it with fault-free materials.

- The supplier has also agreed to guarantee all material will be fault-free next year and improve the speed and reliability of deliveries. In exchange, Aspex has agreed that the unit cost of material will remain the same as last year.

- Aspex will no longer keep stocks of material.

- The costs making up the *cost of quality* will be saved.

Working capital control and other matters

- The unit cost of production labour will remain the same and there will be no change in the remaining fixed overheads.

- The average age of debtors will be 2 months.

- Aspex has agreed that the average age of creditors will be 1 month.

- The cash balance will remain the same. Any surplus cash will be used to pay off the existing loans.

- No fixed assets will be bought or sold during the year to 30 November 2007.

Task 3.2

Prepare the following estimates for the year to 30 November 2007 for Stuart Morgan:

(a)   sales volume

(b)   purchases

(c)   cost of purchases

(d)   selling price per Zeta

(e)   turnover

(f)   total contribution

(g)   fixed costs

(h)   operating profit

(i)   net assets at 30 November 2007

(j)   net profit (or sales) margin

(k)   return on capital employed.

Unit 33
Management
Accounting

Practice examination 2
Cheltenham Ltd, Brown Ltd and LNG Ltd

This examination paper is in THREE sections.

You must show competency in ALL sections.

You should therefore attempt and aim to complete EVERY task in EACH section.

You should spend about 60 minutes on Section 1 and 60 minutes on Section 2 and 60 minutes on Section 3.

Include all essential workings within your answers, where appropriate.

SECTION 1

You should spend about 60 minutes on this section.

DATA

You are employed as an accounting technician with a large firm of accountants and registered auditors. One of your firm's clients is Judith Myers. Judith is the major shareholder in Cheltenham Ltd. Last year she appointed a manager to run the company on her behalf.

The company makes a single product, the Zylo, and the manager has prepared the following operating statement for the year ended 31 May 2006.

Cheltenham Ltd: Budgeted and actual operating statement for the year ended 31 May 2006		
	Budget	*Actual*
Sales volume, Zylos	9,000	8,800
Production volume, Zylos	9,000	10,000
	£	£
Turnover	630,000	616,000
Materials	45,000	52,000
Labour	55,800	65,000
Electricity	38,000	42,000
Depreciation	70,000	65,000
Rent and rates	24,000	25,000
Other fixed overheads	40,000	42,000
Cost of production	272,800	291,000
less closing stock		34,920
Cost of sales	272,800	256,080
Operating profit	357,200	359,920

Judith cannot understand why the actual profit is greater than the budgeted profit despite selling fewer Zylos during the year. The manager gives you the following information.

- All Zylos are sold for the same price.

- Material and labour are variable costs.

- Electricity is a semi-variable cost. The budgeted fixed cost element was £20,000 and the actual fixed cost element was £21,000.

- All other costs are fixed costs.

- The actual closing stocks were valued at their actual variable cost plus an appropriate proportion of production overheads.

- Cheltenham did not buy or sell any fixed assets during the year.

- There were no stocks of work in progress at any time and no opening finished stocks.

Task 1.1

(a)   Calculate the following data per Zylo:

   (i)   budgeted selling price

   (ii)   budgeted material cost

   (iii) budgeted labour cost

   (iv)   budgeted variable cost of electricity

   (v)   actual selling price

   (vi)   actual material cost

   (vii) actual labour cost

   (viii) actual variable cost of electricity

(b)   Prepare a revised operating statement using marginal (or variable) costing to show the flexible budget, the actual results and any variances.

(c)   Add a note to your statement to explain why your actual profit is different from the actual profit prepared by the manager.

SECTION 2

You should spend about 60 minutes on this section.

DATA

Brown Ltd manufactures and sells office furniture. The company operates an integrated standard cost system in which:

•   purchases of materials are recorded at standard cost

•   finished goods are recorded at standard cost

•   direct materials and direct labour costs are both variable costs

•   fixed production overheads are absorbed using direct labour hours

You are an accounting technician at Brown Ltd. You report to Sam Thomas, the Finance Director.

The company's most popular product is an executive desk. Its standard cost is as follows:

Product: Executive Desk			
Inputs	Quantity	Unit Price £	Total cost £
Direct materials	30kgs	5.00	150.00
Direct labour	5 hours	6.00	30.00
Fixed production overheads	5 hours	4.00	20.00
Standard cost			200.00

Actual and budgeted data for the manufacture of executive desks for May 2006 are shown below.

- 27,500 kgs of direct materials were purchased for £143,000.
- Issues from stores to production totalled 27,500 kgs.
- The actual output for the month was 900 desks.
- The budgeted output for the month was 1,000 desks.
- 4,200 direct labour hours were worked at a cost of £26,040.
- Actual fixed production overheads were £23,000.

Task 2.1

(a)   Calculate the following information for May:

   (i)   actual price of materials per kg
   (ii)   standard usage of materials for actual production
   (iii)   actual labour rate per hour
   (iv)   standard labour hours for actual production
   (v)   budgeted production overheads

(b)   Calculate the following variances for the production of executive desks for May:

   (i)   the material price variance
   (ii)   the material usage variance
   (iii)   the labour rate variance
   (iv)   the labour efficiency variance
   (v)   the fixed overhead expenditure variance
   (vi)   the fixed overhead volume variance
   (vii)   the fixed overhead capacity variance
   (viii) the fixed overhead efficiency variance

(c)   Prepare an operating statement for May which reconciles the standard absorption cost of total actual production with the actual absorption cost of total actual production.

(d)   Write a memo for Sam Thomas to present to the Board of Directors. Your memo should comment on the usefulness, or otherwise, of the statement you have prepared in your answer to (c) above.

SECTION 3

You should spend about 60 minutes on this section.

DATA

You work as an accounting technician at LNG Ltd reporting to the Finance Director. LNG prints and publishes newspapers.

Extracts from the latest operating statements of the LNG Ltd and certain performance indicators from its competitor Ads Ltd are shown below.

Profit and loss account extract for the year ended 30 November 2006 LNG Ltd

	£000
Advertising sales	4,200
Less Cost of sales:	
Materials	(1,900)
Direct labour	(430)
Fixed production overheads	(880)
Gross profit	990
Sales and distribution costs	(540)
Administration costs	(240)
Operating profit	210

Balance sheet extract at 30 November 2006

	£000
Fixed assets	3,265
Debtors	1,050
Cash	85
Creditors	(600)
Net assets	3,800

Other operating data	LNG Ltd
Newspapers produced	7,500,000
Number of employees	70
Advertising transactions	40,000

Performance indicators for Ads Ltd	
Gross profit margin	33.2%
Operating profit margin	10.0%
Return on capital employed	15.4%
Debtor age (in months)	2.0
Average revenue per newspaper	£0.75
Advertising revenue per employee	£88,500.00
Advertising revenue per advertising transaction	£120.00

Task 3.1

(a) With reference to the performance indicators for Ads Ltd, briefly explain how benchmarking is used to improve performance.

(b) Calculate the following performance indicators for LNG Ltd:

  (i) gross profit margin

  (ii) operating profit margin

  (iii) return on capital employed

  (iv) average age of debtors in months

  (v) average advertising revenue per newspaper produced

  (vi) advertising revenue per employee

  (vii) average advertising revenue per advertising transaction

ADDITIONAL DATA

At LNG Ltd, a management meeting was held to discuss the annual results. In a bid to increase profits and be more competitive, the following improvements were identified.

- Average advertising revenue per advertising transaction could be increased by 5%.

- Wastage of paper could be reduced which would result in a saving of 3% in total material costs.

- A credit controller could be employed at an annual cost of £25,000. As a result, debtors would be reduced to £850,000.

- Surplus land could be sold for its book value of £500,000 and the proceeds distributed to the shareholders.

Task 3.2

(a) Restate the LNG Ltd profit and loss account for the year ended 30 November 2006, assuming each of the improvements had been implemented on 1 December 2005.

(b) In a memo to the Board of Directors, indicate the overall effect of the improvements on EACH of the performance indicators for LNG Ltd calculated in Task 3.1.

Unit 33
Management
Accounting

Practice examination 3
Jorvik Ltd, Bell plc and Duo Ltd

This examination paper is in THREE sections.

You must show competency in ALL sections.

You should therefore attempt and aim to complete EVERY task in EACH section.

You should spend about 60 minutes on Section 1, 60 minutes on Section 2 and 60 minutes on Section 3.

Include all essential workings within your answers, where appropriate.

SECTION 1

You should spend about 60 minutes on this section.

DATA

You are employed as an accounting technician by Jorvik Ltd, a company that makes several products including one called the Delta. The company operates a five day week for both production and sales, and budgets for the Delta are divided into four-weekly periods. Jorvik has prepared a sales forecast for Deltas for the next five periods. This is shown below.

Period	1	2	3	4	5
Twenty days ending	28 January	25 February	25 March	22 April	21 May
Sales of Deltas	19,200	23,040	28,800	34,560	30,720

Anne Morris is Jorvik's production director. She gives you the following information.

Stocks

- There are no stocks of raw materials or work in progress at the end of any period.
- There are 7,680 Deltas in stock at the beginning of period 1.
- Closing stocks of Deltas must equal 8 days sales volume of the next period.

Production data

- 4% of finished Delta production is found to be faulty on completion.
- Faulty production has no value and has to be destroyed.
- Each Delta requires 2 litres of material.
- Material has to be used in the period it is purchased.

Task 1.1

Prepare the following budgets for EACH of the first four periods:

(a)   production budget showing the numbers of Deltas to be made to achieve the sales forecasts
(b)   material purchases budget in litres

DATA

After you prepared your production and material budgets, Anne Morris tells you that:

- the maximum material available in any four-week period will be 60,000 litres
- Jorvik will allow finished stocks to be greater than 8 days over the first four periods if necessary
- any increase in the amount of stock should be kept to a minimum because of financing costs

Task 1.2

For each of the first four periods, prepare the following:

(a)   a statement showing any shortages or surpluses of materials in each period

(b)   a statement that reschedules any shortages while allowing the sales forecasts to be met and financing costs to be minimised

(c)   a revised material purchases budget in litres

(d)   a revised production budget in units based on the revised material purchases and showing production before and after allowing for the faulty Deltas

DATA

You give Ann Morris your revised production and material budgets. She gives you the following additional information.

Materials

•   Material costs £2.10 per litre.

Labour

•   Five Deltas can be made per labour hour.

•   Jorvik employs 40 production employees who each work a guaranteed 35 hours per five day week.

•   The hourly rate per employee is £6.00 and, if overtime is required, the premium is 50%.

Factory overheads

•   Factory overheads are 150% of the labour cost of production.

•   Any overtime premium is charged to factory overheads.

•   Idle time is also charged to factory overheads.

Task 1.3

Using the revised production budget prepare the following for each of the first four periods:

(a)   cost of material purchases budget

(b)   labour budget in hours

(c)   cost of labour budget broken down into labour charged to production and labour charged to factory overheads

(d)   cost of production budget, including factory overheads

SECTION 2

You should spend about 60 minutes on this section.

DATA

Bell plc manufactures and sells two types of stove, Model F and Model H. You work as an accounting technician reporting to the Finance Director. The company uses a standard cost stock system in which purchases of materials are recorded at standard cost. Fixed production overheads are absorbed using a budgeted overhead absorption rate per labour hour.

The standard production cost for both models was set in January 2006 and is as follows:

	Model F			Model H		
	Quantity	Price £	Total £	Quantity	Price £	Total £
Materials	20 kgs	2.00	40.00	40 kgs	2.00	80.00
Labour	5 hours	5.00	25.00	8 hours	5.00	40.00
Fixed Overheads	5 hours	6.00	30.00	8 hours	6.00	48.00
Standard cost			95.00			168.00

Actual and budgeted data for May 2006 are as follows:

• 350,000 kgs of materials were purchased at a cost of £675,500.

• Issues from stores for the production of Model F were 210,000 kgs

• 52,000 direct labour hours were worked producing Model F at a cost of £254,800.

• Total direct labour hours worked were 58,600.

• Budgeted output for Model F was 10,000 and for Model H was 1,000.

• 9,800 Model F and 1,000 Model H stoves were produced.

• Actual fixed production overheads were £360,000.

• The company had 1,000 Model F and 500 Model H stoves in stock on both 1 May and 31 May.

Task 2.1

(a)   Calculate the following information for May:

    (i)   the actual price of materials per kg

    (ii)   the standard usage of materials for Model F

    (iii)   the standard hours for the production of Model F

    (iv)   the actual direct labour hour rate for producing Model F

    (v)   the budgeted fixed production overheads

(b)   Calculate the following variances for May:

   (i)   the materials price variance

   (ii)   the fixed overhead expenditure variance

   (iii)   the fixed overhead volume variance

   (iv)   the fixed overhead capacity variance

   (v)   the fixed overhead efficiency variance

(c)   Calculate for the production of the Model F stove for May:

   (i)   the materials usage variance

   (ii)   the labour rate variance

   (iii)   the labour efficiency variance

ADDITIONAL DATA

The Purchasing Department has provided the following data for the purchase of materials for January to April:

	Quantity Purchased	Price Variance
	kgs	£
January	200,000	4,000 (F)
February	250,000	10,000 (F)
March	280,000	11,200 (F)
April	300,000	18,000 (F)

Task 2.2

(a)   Calculate the actual price of materials per kg for each of the four months to April.

(b)   Write a memo to the Finance Director in which you:

   (i)   identify the movement in material prices over the four months

   (ii)   explain TWO possible reasons for this movement

   (iii)   identify ONE effect this movement in material prices might have on the Purchasing Department and any implications it has for the company

SECTION 3

You should spend about 60 minutes on this section.

DATA

Duo Ltd owns two factories, A and B, which make and sell furniture to customers' orders. Each factory has its own general manager who is responsible for sales policy, pricing and purchasing. The forecasts for both factories for the year ending 31 December 2007 are shown below.

Profit and loss account extract for the year ending 31 December 2007		
	Factory A	Factory B
	£000	£000
Turnover	2,200	2,850
Materials	660	784
Direct labour	440	448
Fixed production overheads	220	420
Cost of sales	1,320	1,652
Gross profit	880	1,198
Sales and distribution costs	(520)	(640)
Administration costs	(210)	(250)
Operating profit	150	308

Balance sheet extract at 31 December 2007		
	£000	£000
Fixed assets	1,255	7,410
Stocks	120	142
Debtors	183	238
Cash	2	10
Creditors	(60)	(100)
Net assets	1,500	7,700
Other data		
Units produced and sold	22,000	30,000
Budgeted labour hours	75,000	85,000

The following information is also relevant:

- Stocks comprise raw materials for both factories.

- Stocks will remain unchanged throughout the year.

- The amount for trade creditors relates only to purchases of stocks.

- Factory A has a capacity of 70,000 labour hours and Factory B 140,000 labour hours.

- Sales and distribution costs are variable with turnover from each factory.

- Administration costs are fixed.

Task 3.1

Using the forecast financial information, calculate the following performance indicators, to one decimal place, for both factories:

(a)   gross profit margin

(b)   operating profit margin

(c)   return on capital employed

(d)   stock turnover in months (note that stock value is based on materials cost only)

(e)   age of creditors in months

(f)   age of debtors in months

(g)   labour capacity ratio

Unit 33
Management
Accounting

Practice examination 4
CityEng Ltd, LNG Ltd and Bell plc

This examination paper is in THREE sections.

You must show competency in ALL sections.

You should therefore attempt and aim to complete EVERY task in EACH section.

You should spend about 60 minutes on Section 1 and 60 minutes on Section 2 and 60 minutes on Section 3.

Include all essential workings within your answers, where appropriate.

SECTION 1

You should spend about 60 minutes on this section.

DATA

You are employed as a management accountant by CityEng Ltd and you report to Tara Williams, CityEng's Finance Director. CityEng makes a single product, the M9, which it sells to only one customer, Car Makers plc. The M9 is a precision product and Car Makers demands high levels of quality control.

When preparing the budgets for the year ending 31 May 2006, it was not certain what the demand would be for the M9. Because of that CityEng developed two possible plans. The first plan, plan A, assumed demand for the M9 would be 300,000 units: the second plan, plan B, assumed demand would be 400,000 units.

Both plans are shown below, together with the actual operating results of CityEng for the year ended 31 May 2006.

CityEng Ltd: planned and actual operating results year ended 31 May 2006			
	Plan A	Plan B	Actual results
Volume	300,000	400,000	380,000
	£000	£000	£000
Turnover	6,900	9,200	8,626
Material	2,400	3,200	3,116
Labour	1,500	2,000	1,938
Semi-variable cost: electricity	1,400	1,800	1,624
Stepped cost: quality control	360	480	358
Fixed cost: rent and rates	200	200	200
Fixed cost: depreciation	400	400	100
Operating profit	640	1,120	1,290

Notes to the planned operating results

- Both plans assumed the same unit selling price, the same unit variable (or marginal) costs and the same fixed costs.

- Both material and labour are variable (or marginal) costs.

- Quality control includes supervision. It is a stepped cost. The cost increases by the same amount for every 100,000 – or part of 100,000 – M9s produced.

Notes to the actual operating results

- Car Makers needed 420,000 M9s during the year.

- For technical reasons, the same amount of electricity is required for each M9 and no economies are possible.

- There is only one possible electricity supplier for CityEng Ltd. For the year to 31 May 2006 the electricity supplier reduced both its fixed charge and its variable charge per unit of electricity.

Task 1.1

(a)   Calculate the budgeted selling price per M9.

(b)   Calculate the budgeted variable cost per M9 of:

     (i)   material

     (ii)   labour

     (iii)   electricity

(c)   Calculate the budgeted fixed cost of electricity.

(d)   Prepare a statement showing the flexible budget, the actual results and any variances.

DATA

Tara Williams tells you that the company introduced performance-related pay in June 2005 for its senior managers. She believed this could be the reason why the actual profit was greater than forecast under plan B.

Task 1.2

Write a memo to Tara Williams. In your memo you should identify:

(a)   THREE reasons, other than performance related pay, to explain why CityEng's actual profit for the year was greater than planned.

(b)   FOUR general conditions necessary for performance related pay to successfully lead to improved performance in organisations.

SECTION 2

You should spend about 60 minutes on this section.

DATA

You work as an accounting technician at LNG Ltd reporting to the Finance Director. LNG Ltd prints and publishes newspapers. The company operates an integrated standard cost system which:

- purchases of materials are recorded at standard cost

- direct materials and direct labour costs are both variable costs

- all production overheads are fixed and are absorbed using direct labour hours

The standard cost for printing 1,000 newspapers is as follows:

Product:	Newspaper			
Standard quantity:	1,000			
Inputs		*Quantity*	*Unit Price £*	*Total Cost £*
Paper		200 kgs	0.50	100.00
Ink		40 litres	4.00	160.00
Direct labour		10 hours	6.00	60.00
Fixed production overheads		10 hours	12.00	120.00
Standard cost				440.00

Actual and budgeted data for November are as follows.

• 23,200 litres of ink were purchased and used at a cost of £95,120.

• Actual output for the month was 600,000 newspapers.

• The budgeted output for the month was 560,000 newspapers.

• 6,200 direct labour hours were worked at a cost of £38,440.

• Actual fixed production overheads were £70,000.

Task 2.1

(a) Calculate the following information for November:

   (i) actual price of ink per litre

   (ii) standard usage of ink for actual production

   (iii) actual labour rate per hour

   (iv) standard labour hours for actual production

   (v) budgeted production overheads

(b) Calculate the following variances for November:

   (i) price variance for ink

   (ii) usage variance for ink

   (iii) labour rate variance

   (iv) labour efficiency variance

   (v) fixed overhead expenditure variance

   (vi) fixed overhead volume variance

   (vii) fixed overhead capacity variance

   (viii) fixed overhead efficiency variance

(c) Prepare a statement for November which reconciles the fixed overheads incurred with the fixed overheads absorbed in production.

ADDITIONAL DATA

Paper supplies are imported and invoiced in US dollars. Following investigation, you discover that the standard cost for paper was set in July when the exchange rate between the UK pound and the US dollar was $1.80 = £1.00. In November, the company purchased 130,000 kgs of paper for US$110,565 at a sterling cost of £58,500.

Task 2.2

(a)   (i)   Calculate the percentage decrease in the value of the dollar between July and November.

       (ii)   Calculate the material price variance in UK pounds for paper for November.

       (iii)   Subdivide the material price variance for paper showing which part is due to changes in the dollar exchange rate and which part is due to other factors.

(b)   Write a note to the Finance Director which considers whether the price variance due to changes in the dollar exchange rate should be included or excluded from the Purchasing Manager's performance report.

SECTION 3

You should spend about 60 minutes on this section.

DATA

Bell plc manufactures and sells two types of stove, Model F and Model H. You work as an accounting technician reporting to the Finance Director. At the May management meeting the following information relating to Models F and H stoves for April 2006 was presented.

	Model F		Model H	
	Actual	Budget	Actual	Budget
Units sold	10,100	9,800	850	900
Units produced	10,000	10,000	1,000	1,000
Direct labour hours	50,200	50,000	7,800	8,000

	Model F		Model H	
	Actual	Budget	Actual	Budget
	£	£	£	£
Turnover	1,010,000	980,000	187,000	198,000
Standard variable costs	(656,500)	(637,000)	(102,000)	(108,000)
Variable cost variances	(19,500)	-	19,000	-
Contribution	334,000	343,000	104,000	90,000
Fixed production overheads	(294,000)	(294,000)	(43,200)	(43,200)
Gross profit	40,000	49,000	60,800	46,800

Task 3.1

(a)   Calculate the following performance indicators for Model F and Model H for April:

     (i)   budgeted contribution margin

     (ii)   actual contribution margin

     (iii)   budgeted gross profit margin

     (iv)   actual gross profit margin

     (v)   actual capacity ratio

     (vi)   actual efficiency ratio

(b)   Using these indicators and other available data, write a memo to the Managing Director. You should:

(i)   suggest THREE ways to improve the actual gross profit margin for Model F and indicate the feasibility of each

(ii)   identify and explain TWO limitations of using the gross profit margin indicator for decision making purposes.

DATA

Bell plc makes another product called the Omega. One of your tasks is to develop quarterly sales forecasts for the Omega. Quarter 1 represents the three months ending 31 March; quarter 2, the three months ending 30 June; quarter 3, the three months ending 30 September; and quarter 4, the three months ending 31 December.

Bell plc uses the linear regression formula $y = a + bx$ to forecast Omega sales volumes in each quarter. In the formula, y represents the trend, a is a constant and b is the slope of the regression line. The regression formula is based on data for the last nine years and so the value of x for the fourth quarter of 2006, the three months ending 31 December 2006, is 36.

The values used for forecasting Omega sales volumes are:

*   a = 10,000

*   b = 400

*   x = the quarter number

Your manager suggests you should build a spreadsheet model to forecast sales volumes. She tells you that the seasonal variation for the first quarter of 2007, the three months ending 31 March 2007, is +500 and the seasonal variation for the second quarter, the three months ending 30 June 2007, is −1,000.

Task 3.2

Calculate the formulae for the trend and sales volume forecasts for the first two quarters of 2005 to be inserted in cells B7 to C8.

	A	B	C
1	a	10000	
2	b	400	
3	x at 31 December 2006	36	
4	Period	3 months to 31 March 2007	3 months to 30 June 2007
5	Quarter	1	2
6	Seasonal variation	+500	-1000
7	Trend = y		
8	Forecast		

Calculate the formulae to be used in these cells

Unit 33
Management
Accounting

Practice examination 5

Goodman Ltd

This exam is in THREE sections.

Time permitted is 3 hours + 15 minutes reading time.

You have to show competence in all sections.

You should therefore attempt and aim to complete EVERY task in all three sections.

You should spend about 60 minutes on Section 1; 60 minutes on Section 2; and 60 minutes on Section 3. Include all essential workings within your answers, where appropriate.

This practice examination for Unit 33 is reproduced by kind permission of AAT, who have stated: "Please note that although this specimen falls into three sections, this is just to illustrate the type of tasks that may be used to assess the different elements of the standards. Live papers may not feature three sections."

SECTION 1

You should spend about 60 minutes on this section.

THE SITUATION

You are employed by Goodman Ltd as an accounting technician. You report to the Management Accountant. The date is 30th September 2006 and the data and tasks that follow relate to analysis of data before this date and to planning activities after it.

DATA

One of your responsibilities is to help prepare budgets for the company's profit centres. One of these profit centres manufactures and sells product XP6, for which the sales forecast for the next five accounting periods is shown below.

Sales forecast for XP6 to 28/4/07

Accounting period ending	11/11/06	23/12/06	3/2/07	17/3/07	28/4/07
	Period 1	Period 2	Period 3	Period 4	Period 5
Sales volume (units)	36,000	37,500	39,000	42,000	42,000

The following information is also available:

Production

- there are six weeks in each accounting period and the profit centre works a five day week in each of these weeks

- the opening finished stock for period 1 will be 14,400 units

- the current policy of Goodman Ltd is that finished stocks in each period must equal 9 working days sales volume of the next period

Material

- the company operates a Just-In-Time system for raw material purchases, and so there are no raw material stocks

- each unit of XP6 requires 4kgs of material

- there is a 2% wastage of material due to QA inspection failures before material is issued to production

- the profit centre has a contract to purchase up to 160,000 kgs of material in any six week accounting period at a price of £4.00 per kg; all purchases of material beyond the contracted level have to be bought from other sources at a cost of £6.00 per kg

Labour

- it takes 3 labour hours to produce one unit of XP6

- there are 550 production employees in the profit centre

- production employees work a guaranteed, 35 hour, five day week at a weekly wage of £245.00

- any overtime required is payable at £10.00 per hour

Task 1.1

You are required to prepare the following budgets (to the nearest whole number) for EACH of the four periods 1 to 4:

(a)   production budget in units of XP6

(b)   purchases budget in kgs

(c)   cost of purchases budget

(d)   labour budget in hours

(e)   cost of labour budget

DATA

The Operations Director has now reviewed your budget calculations and tells you that the budgeted profit is not at an acceptable level. This is partly because in some periods the company is buying raw materials beyond the level contracted for, and paying a premium for these extra materials by buying on the open market.

As a result, the policy on finished stocks is to be amended. As at present, there must always be sufficient stocks to meet customer needs, therefore, closing stocks cannot be less than 9 days. However, if cost savings can be made, closing stocks can now be more than 9 days. This would involve producing more XP6 than required in some periods in order to make savings in later periods.

Task 1.2

(a)   Based on the current production budget, you are required to prepare the following REVISED budgets for each of the periods 1 to 4 to maximise the material cost savings, taking account of the amended stock policy:

      (i)   purchases budget in kgs

      (ii)   cost of purchases budget

(b)   Write a memo to the Operations Director in which you:

      (i)   calculate the total cost savings achievable by adjusting the raw materials budget

      (ii)   identify TWO possible extra costs that might be incurred as a result of the amended stock policy

SECTION 2

You should spend about 60 minutes on this section.

DATA

Another of your responsibilities is to prepare and monitor standard costing variances. Mixing Department No. 4 mixes raw materials and places these in containers, for use in subsequent production.

Fixed overheads are charged to production on the basis of machine hours, because the machine hours required determines the speed of production. The department operates a continuous process.

The budgeted and actual results of Mixing Department No. 4 for the week ended 30 September 2006 are shown below.

		Budget		**Actual**
Production		5,000 containers		4,800 containers
		Standard cost		Actual cost
Material	25,000 litres	£175,000	23,040 litres	£172,800
Labour	20,000 labour hours	£160,000	20,160 labour hours	£165,312
Fixed overheads	40,000 machine hours	£500,000	37,920 machine hours	£371,616
Total cost		£835,000		£709,728

Task 2.1

(a)   You are required to calculate the following information

(i)   standard price of material per litre

(ii)   actual price of material per litre

(iii)   standard litres of material per containers

(iv)   standard labour rate per hour

(v)   standard labour hours per container

(vi)   standard machine hours per container

(vii)   budgeted fixed overheads per budgeted machine hour

(viii) standard absorption cost per container.

(b)   Using the data provided in the operating results and your answers to part (a), calculate the following variances:

(i)   material price variance

(ii)   material usage variance

(iii)   labour rate variance

(iv)   labour efficiency variance

(v)   fixed overhead expenditure variance

(vi)   fixed overhead volume variance

(vii)   fixed overhead capacity variance

(viii)   fixed overhead efficiency variance

(c)   Prepare a statement reconciling the standard absorption cost of actual operations to the actual absorption cost of actual operations.

(d)   Give TWO possible reasons why each of the following variances may have occurred:

   (i)   material price variance

   (ii)   material usage variance

   (iii)   labour rate variance

   (iv)   fixed overhead volume variance

SECTION 3

You should spend about 60 minutes on this section.

DATA

One of Goodman Ltd's profit centres has the following Income Statement and Balance Sheet extracts relating to the past half-year.

Operating statement for the half-year ended 30 September 2006		
	£000	*£000*
Turnover		20,000
Material	9,260	
Labour	3,960	
Production fixed overheads	1,580	
Cost of production	14,800	
Add opening finished stock	400	
Less closing finished stock	(3,700)	
Cost of sales		11,500
Gross profit		8,500
Research and development	1,776	
Training	2,220	
Customer support	600	
Marketing	1,200	
Administration	1,104	6,900
Net operating profit		1,600

Extract from Balance Sheet at 30 September 2006		
	£000	£000
Fixed assets		
Machinery and equipment		
Cost		12,000
Accumulated depreciation		(4,000)
Net book value		8,000
Net current assets		
Stock of finished goods	2,650	
Debtors	5,000	
Cash	(2,400)	
Creditors	(3,250)	2,000
Net assets		10,000

Task 3.1

You are required to prepare the following performance indicators:

(a)   gross profit margin

(b)   net profit (operating) margin

(c)   return on capital employed

(d)   fixed asset turnover

(e)   average age of debtors in months

(f)   research and development as a percentage of the cost of production

(g)   training as a percentage of the cost of production

(h)   customer support as a percentage of turnover

Task 3.2

Explain the significance of the following ratios:

(a)   Fixed asset turnover

(b)   Return on capital employed

DATA

The Management Accountant has suggested that the use of the Balanced Scorecard will help in the analysis of Goodman Ltd's performance.

Task 3.3

You are required to prepare a Memo to the Management Accountant in which you:

•   explain the advantages of a Balanced Scorecard approach

•   identify ONE balanced scorecard perspective being measured for each of the performance indicators derived in task 3.1